D0526529

WITHDRAWN
FROM
UNIVERSITY
OF
GREENWICH
LIBRARY

798

Forgive no error you recognize,
it will repeat itself, increase,
and afterwards our pupils
will not forgive in us what we forgave.

Lines from 'Lies' by Yevgeny
Yevtushenko, by kind permission of Penguin
Books Ltd.

Sometimes I squeeze my letters together and I don't realize it like this; Fast

This is my very neat hanwriting, but I can't write like this unless I go very slowly.

Speed and spacing suffer when writers think that separate letters are neat.

This is my best writing, but it takes too long.

This is my essay writing, it doesn't take as long.

This is my scribble, I use it for creative writing. it still ensn't fast enough for my thoughts.

This is my printed scribble, I also use it for and it is about as fast as my scribble writing painful because I grip the pen to hard and probably as well. I'm usually the only one who can read miss out parts of letters such as · on the eyes

Continuous cursive can be inefficient and does not easily speed up.

This is probably something like my best

my roughest fast writing.

Neat print is slow and immature. The rough writing is efficient and adult.

We need flexible, efficient handwriting. These pupils' comments, as well as their letterforms, show how the concept of neat, best handwriting can be counter-productive.

Handwriting

a new perspective

Rosemary Sassoon

Stanley Thornes (Publishers) Limited

CON 134586
9.99
BC 249050

This book reflects my observations and research after more than ten years in the field of handwriting. My views on such matters as the effect of posture on the written trace, and the influence of models in the widest sense, were formed many years ago. Training as a classical scribe, followed by a career designing and teaching letterforms led me to consider the balance between discipline and creativity as crucial. In everyday handwriting too, essential skill training must precede but should never override the desirable personal aspects of the written trace.

Handwriting is an emotive and complex subject so I would not expect everyone to agree with all my ideas. When I started looking at handwriting problems few people had given much thought to the subject; now it is becoming a popular study. I hope that this book will encourage practitioners and researchers to look more deeply into all aspects of handwriting and not be satisfied with facile solutions. The conclusions that I have drawn are what I feel right for this time, but we all need to be sensitive to an ever-changing situation.

I would like to thank all the teachers who helped me in my work. Many shared their ideas or undertook surveys on in-service courses, without even giving their names, so it is not possible to thank them, or their pupils, individually. I would like to express my gratitude to my indefatigable editor, Roger Crowley, and to Pat Savage whose line drawings add so much to my books, not forgetting my husband John and daughter Caroline, who share my ideals and support me in so many ways.

Rosemary Sassoon

Text © Rosemary Sassoon 1990

Original line illustrations © Pat Savage 1990

All rights reserved. No part of this publication may be reproduced or transmitted in any form or by any means, electronic or mechanical, including photocopy, recording, or any information storage and retrieval system, without permission in writing from the publisher or under licence from the Copyright Licensing Agency Limited. Further details of such licences (for reprographic reproduction) may be obtained from the Copyright Licensing Agency Limited, of 33–4 Alfred Place, London WC1E 7DP.

First published in 1990 by:
Stanley Thornes (Publishers) Ltd
Old Station Drive
Leckhampton
CHELTENHAM GL53 0DN
England

Cover design and photo by
Gunnlaugur SE Briem.

British Library Cataloguing in Publication Data

Sassoon, Rosemary
    Handwriting, a new perspective.
    1. Children. Curriculum subjects: Handwriting. Teaching
    I. Title
    745.6'1'07

ISBN 0-7487-0167-2

Typeset by Tech-Set, Gateshead, Tyne & Wear.
Printed and bound in Great Britain at The Bath Press, Avon.

Contents

PART 1 A new way of thinking about handwriting

1   Why handwriting matters   1

2   The changing role of handwriting – different levels for different tasks   3

3   Handwriting is the visible trace of a hand movement   7

4   The concepts behind our alphabet   11

5   How you write in terms of posture is as important as what you write in
    terms of letters   16

6   A systematic teaching method is needed – not necessarily a strict model   23

7   Suggestions for curriculum planning   25

8   The case for a consistent terminology   29

PART 2 A new way of looking at handwriting

9   The role of surveys and research   33

10   Looking at handwriting from different angles   37

11   Looking at the movement of letters   39

12   Looking at joins   44

13   Looking at handwriting models   53

14   Looking at speed   59

15   Looking at pencils and pens   61

16   Looking at penhold and taking pain into consideration   66

17   Looking at posture and paper position   70

18   Recommendations from research into children's handwriting   73

PART 3 A new way of looking at handwriting problems

19   Handwriting as a diagnostic tool   75

20   Problems that show through handwriting   77

21   Specific problems for left-handers   79

22   Problems with directionality   83

23   Perceptual problems   86

24   Observing, assessing and dealing with tremors   89

25   Fatigue   92

26   Gaps in learning   94

27   Posture as an indicator, as well as a cause of problems   95

28   An attitude of understanding   97

     Index   98

PART 1

A new way of thinking about handwriting

If handwriting is to survive as a skill, systematic yet imaginative ways of teaching the basics are essential. Consideration must also be given to the letterforms that would promote efficiency and to factors that affect handwriting posture. To work properly, handwriting must be automatic. For this to happen, most aspects from pen and penhold, to the model or degree of joining should eventually be the choice of the writer. Before these concepts can be accepted, a lot of preconceived ideas will have to alter, replacing them perhaps with the thought that handwriting must suit both writer and reader.

If we recognise the necessity to teach the basic skill, but not always to insist on neatness or uniformity then children should profit by evolving efficient handwriting that will serve them well at speed. If we respect the individuality of children's choice, and accept the fact that differences in handwriting are not a disadvantage but often the opposite (and for some children the only way they can write), then we may assist a new generation to acquire a relaxed command of what is still the most immediate form of graphic communication.

1 Why handwriting matters

Handwriting is still an essential skill, despite modern technology. People present themselves to the world through their handwriting, and are inevitably judged by it. From our earliest school days, success and failure are often measured in terms of neat handwriting. Parents eagerly await these first visible results of learning; comparisons are made and judgements begin to be formed, often with little understanding of the issues involved. Children who cannot write well soon realise their lack of success by comparing their own performance with other children's. If they are criticised too much, this may only make matters worse. The constant visible reminder of failure can affect the writer's self-image in a subtle and destructive way. Handwriting problems can lead to underachievement in all written work and influence children's attitudes and behaviour throughout the school. These are all reasons why handwriting matters so much.

This is my normal handwriting

This is my fastest handwriting

*This is my script handwriting
I can not do (And I hate.)*

I LIKE TO WRITE LIKE THIS, TOO.

Good writing, whatever the model, has natural rhythm and character.

At an adult level, more subtle judgements about educational attainment and character may be formed from handwriting. People for whom neatness is important, may like others to be neat and to have neat handwriting. Practical people may themselves have developed an efficient handwriting and be put off by writers with an over-decorative script, whereas highly creative people might be attracted to a writing that reflects imaginative or artistic qualities. People can be predisposed to like or dislike others before they have even met them, because handwriting is a reflection of the writer on paper.

These personal attitudes complicate the issue of how to teach handwriting and mean that it can never be as straightforward as teaching more factual subjects. If pupils are unable or unwilling to reproduce the handwriting that is expected of them, considerable antagonism can arise. Such feelings may not be conscious on the part of any adults involved, but they must be faced. The subject of handwriting demands a practical and unemotional approach if all our children's needs are to be met.

Looking at handwriting from the writer's angle

This book aims to look at some of the established beliefs and views on handwriting and to suggest ways in which our thinking about the subject needs to develop. For those of us concerned with children – teachers, parents, psychologists or therapists – a first step might be to reassess our own position and attempt to look at handwriting more from the child's point of view. This does not mean being child-led, rather it points to a need for decisions that take children's long-term requirements into account. Handwriting matters because, for most children, it affects so much of what they do almost every day of their school life.

It may be necessary to change some of the attitudes that have served us well in the past but are not so relevant today. The overriding priority in bringing about these changes must be first of all a far wider and deeper knowledge of all aspects of the subject.

2 The changing role of handwriting – different levels for different tasks

Handwriting as we know it, has developed throughout history, constantly altering in its usage as well as in details of letterforms and writing implements. Different letterforms have usually resulted from the development of pens but the invention of printing and then, centuries later, the coming of the typewriter, both resulted in changes in the usage of handwriting. The development of computers for use in the classroom, home and office presents us with another new situation. In order to understand our contemporary requirements, it is helpful to look briefly at some of the historical perspectives in the handwriting that we have inherited.

Lines from a copybook, written by Eliza Cox in 1852.

Historical influences on letters

Individually, handwriting reflects partly what children have been taught (or not taught for that matter) and partly what they are. Collectively, handwriting has usually reflected the educational policy and social history of an age. People often ask, 'why do we not write as beautifully as our grandparents?' The answer reflects a difference in both our social requirements and our writing implements between then and now.

Before typewriters were in general use in offices, handwriting had above all to be legible. The elementary school system was a training ground for clerks in the nineteenth century. Much of the curriculum was devoted to teaching the complex movement of copperplate handwriting, to the detriment of creative work. This graceful writing was a product not only of the pens available at that time, but of ceaseless practice and a desire, as well as a need, for conformity. The pen, the penhold and the handwriting model, differed considerably from those used today. These three factors are usually interdependent.

Historically, when one has altered for whatever reason, the other two have also tended to change. The influence of pens on the resulting letterforms was particularly important. When using a pointed quill (or later a steel pen) to write copperplate, the ink flow had to be started with a gentle upstroke otherwise the pen would split open and blot. For the same reason, a writer would not risk stopping in the middle of a word, so the hand rested lightly on the table, perhaps just supported on the little finger. In this way, it could glide easily across the page. This method resulted in a continuous cursive writing that is still copied by many countries without their understanding the factors that influenced the development of such letters. Speed, even for clerks, was not as necessary as legibility and conformity. A 'good, clear hand' was an invaluable asset for an employee. It was also the mark of an educated man or woman in a more leisurely age where letter-writing was an art.

Today we need to write at speed as well as legibly

Keyboards may soon take over some of the chores that face our older pupils, but handwriting will continue to be an essential skill, and how it is used in schools needs careful consideration. Writing has to be legible, but increasingly speed is the top priority. The time has come to understand that there should be different levels of legibility depending on both the task and the reader. If, for instance, writers are producing something that they alone will read, then as long as they can decipher it, that is enough.

What a writer considers to be neat may not always be legible, as the second writer points out.

Handwriting at secondary level involves copying large quantities of notes at top speed and many tasks are undertaken in conditions of stress. Essays for examinations and homework alike, are assessed and are likely to affect pupils' futures. Therefore a great deal of the average teenager's written work takes place under pressure. The effects of such tension need to be taken into consideration. It may be that with the added requirement of continuous legibility, and often neatness as well, we are expecting too much of our hands. They are being asked to perform a precision task, at speed and under tension. For older students this activity continues out of school hours, in the evening and during the weekends as well. There are several different ways of alleviating this problem. Note-taking could be reduced by giving résumés of some lessons. These could be spaced on the page in such a way that pupils could enlarge on essential topics. Alternatively, pupils could be taught techniques for taking down important points in diagrammatic form, for enlarging on later. Older pupils can be allowed to produce some of their homework on a typewriter or word processor, but if this is not possible, the accent on neatness will have to be relaxed. Those accustomed to reading teenagers' scripts soon develop techniques for deciphering them. Examiners may take off a few marks in exasperation when confronted with a near-illegible paper, but pupils are likely to lose a larger percentage if they write too slowly in the mistaken belief that neatness will gain them marks. There can be no marks for what has not been written down at all. A sensible and flexible attitude is needed to balance speed and legibility in different situations.

When pupils are encouraged to produce examples of fast, slow, best or neatest writing, their comments as well as the difference in the letterforms show how important it is to encourage different levels of handwriting. See the examples on the frontispiece.

To sum up the matter briefly, it will be observed that a clever person cares very little about the form of his writing – it is the matter alone which concerns him; whereas, with a limited brainpower, great care as to appearance is taken. But human nature is never a simple combination of elements, it is dependable upon a complexity of changes and chances.

From Thoyts E.E., *How to Decipher Old Documents* (Elliot Stock, 1893).

We need to clarify our own attitudes to handwriting

One of the consequences of this situation is the importance of accepting that it is neither possible nor desirable to have perfect handwriting all the time. Children should be encouraged at quite an early age to have several levels of handwriting at school. They may need a slow 'show' handwriting in certain situations but note-taking and drafting hands not only can, but should be, less time-consuming than 'special occasion' hands. Calligraphic standards of handwriting cannot be maintained at speed, so starting pupils off with too high an expectation of writing may be almost as damaging as too low an expectation. They may find it difficult later to relax their standards sufficiently to get enough written down in examinations. It is essential, therefore, that we are clear about the standards we require of children and the reasons for asking them. This more flexible perspective may also have implications for schools. Fast, relaxed writing and slow, neat handwriting may need different teaching methods. Teaching needs to take into account the realities that older children face.

In effect, modern technology has supplied many alternative means of recording and transmitting information, so we must take a different and more practical look at the remaining essential uses of handwriting. The written trace remains the most personal and immediate means of graphic communication. It must meet the requirements of both reader and writer, so it must be legible enough to serve the reader and fast enough to serve the writer. Between these two, however, there is plenty of room for flexibility.

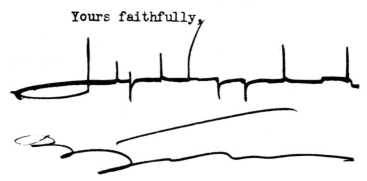

A signature is the one usage of handwriting that needs to be consistent but not necessarily legible. Examples from a collection of illegible signatures belonging to Kathleen Strange.

We must accept a measure of individuality

Recognition of the need to accept children's individuality must follow. Children are encouraged to be creative from their earliest school days, so this individuality will, and should be, echoed in their handwriting. After all, adults vary enormously in their writing; the more creative they are the more interesting a handwriting they may have, and provided it is legible, this is an advantage. Handwriting is a product of our hands, so the individual way in which we use our bodies will be echoed in our handwriting. For a fast but legible handwriting, that is also relaxed and pain-free to produce, both penhold and letters need to be appropriate for modern pens.

Handwriting has to be automated in order to work properly for the writer, and the sooner this happens the better. It is of course essential that the basic skill of handwriting should be taught and taught systematically. The correct movement of letters and the few but essential conventions that determine the legibility of our alphabet, such as height differentials, are vital, but maybe some of the less important aspects that are a matter of personal taste should not be so strictly imposed. It might, for example, be better if children did not have to think about details of slant or proportion of individual letters when concentrating on the content of their written work. We should be trying to train communicators who write legibly, but in a way suited to their own hands and personality, not forgers who can slavishly imitate an impersonal style. One of the aims of this book is to separate those aspects of writing that it is essential to teach if we are to have an efficient means of communicating, from those that are best left to develop in an individual way.

3 Handwriting is the visible trace of a hand movement

A crucial shift in perspective that I wish to stress, is that the emphasis in handwriting should be less on neatness and more on movement, particularly in the early stages. Neatness is usually the first priority in schools and sometimes it is the only one where handwriting is concerned. It is not easy to change this strongly held conviction and explain why the emphasis from the start should be put on the correct movement of letters. It means looking on handwritten letters in a different way and appreciating that they are the visible trace of a hand movement.

It is the hand that has to be trained in the correct movement of each letter. The motor memory controls movements and it soon automates the action of the hand. Once this has happened the actual direction of each letter is retrieved automatically as the writer requires it. If the point of entry or the direction of the strokes that govern the movement of individual letters have been incorrectly automated then it will be difficult for the writer to alter them. This explains why children who have learned to write not much more than their names before they come to school, but who have got used to using letters that do not move correctly, have such difficulty in changing to letters with a correct movement. This underlines the importance of having a systematic handwriting policy that stresses the importance of movement. It also points to the desirability of keeping parents and pre-school groups informed.

The correct movement of basic letters is vital, particularly in names where children first experiment. Kevin's and Paul's writing illustrate the dangers of joining before all letters move correctly.

Towards letters that move efficiently

A second, strongly held belief that needs to be questioned is the use of print script. The letters that children are first taught at school are going to affect them for a long time. These letters need to be suitable for developing into an efficient handwriting later on in school life. Such letters must eventually allow the hand to flow smoothly and quickly across the page leaving a legible trace behind. For nearly fifty years now, simplified straight letters called print script in Great Britain, and sometimes by different names in other countries, have been used to introduce children to writing. Before that, young children were taught a copperplate-based cursive from the beginning, so it is understandable

Three models based on different concepts:

1 Ball and stick, static letters drawn in separate strokes.

2 Fairbank, the arches move but there are no exit strokes.

3 Briem, letters that express a forward movement.

that something simpler was sought. At almost the same time, Marion Richardson was developing her simplified cursive, and that might have been a more satisfactory route to follow. The problem with print script is that it trains children to make an abrupt movement where all the pressure is on the finishing point at the baseline. The more carefully children train their hands to produce these neat straight letters, the more difficult it may be for them to relax and develop the flowing movement that is necessary for any joins to occur. Much of the research that supports the retention of print script takes place in the United States, where the only alternative model in most schools is the same kind of complex cursive handwriting that was taught up until 1930 in Great Britain.

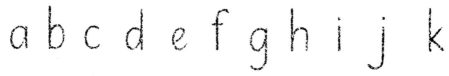

Print script from Smith and Inglis, *New Nelson Teacher's Manual* (Nelson, 1984).

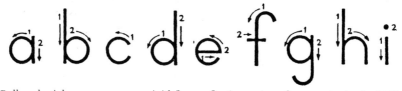

Ball and stick, an even more rigid form of print script often taught in the USA.

Sat upon a rail
Niddle Naddle
Went his head

Neat print script letters at eight years old.

winter is the king of snowtime
Turning tree stumps into snow men
And houses into birthday cakes

Straight letters with no signs of joins at eleven years old.

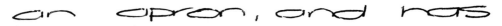

Immature printing at the age of fifteen.

The alternative to print script

The remedy to this situation is simple, and costs nothing in the way of expensive copy-books or extensive teacher training. The addition of exit strokes to the base of the first letters that children are taught, trains them in just the right movement. This encourages spontaneous joins along the baseline as children's letters get closer together and are written more quickly. Exit strokes build in a natural space between letters and ensure that the hand moves in the best trajectory, whether the pencil is lifted to produce separate letters or is left on the paper to result in a join.

abcdefghijklmnopqrstuvwxyz

Letters with exit strokes Gordon and Mock, *Twentieth Century Handwriting* (Methuen, 1960).

iltu rnmhbpk cadgqoe

Letters with exit strokes Sassoon R., *Handwriting: the way to teach it* (Stanley Thornes, 1990).

Jesus went to Jerusalem all of
Dear Rachel
I hope you have a good time
Learn to read I hope you
a nice dinner area we

Four examples from one reception class where exit strokes are taught from the start. They show how easily infants can learn to join.

Letters with exit strokes are increasingly being used in schools in Great Britain. They are spreading effortlessly as the beneficial example of those who have already made the change becomes apparent to others searching for a better way of teaching handwriting. Some teachers still raise two points in defence of print script. Firstly that print script is easier to teach. In the first instance that may be true, but this new way of looking at handwriting takes into account what is best for children later on. Exit strokes ensure a smoother progression to a relaxed flowing hand. This new attitude also points out that what is good for most children may not succeed with everyone. If one or two young children in any group are having real difficulty in dealing with exit strokes, then they should be allowed to start with straight letters but go on to those with exits as soon as they are able.

The second argument in defence of print script is that children need to write letters that look like those they see in their reading books. Most children learn to recognise a variety of forms of letters very quickly from television graphics, advertisements and many other sources. Many different typefaces are in fact used in early reading material, and the move towards a 'real books approach' to reading, where children meet with many different typographic conventions from the start, is a recognition of this. However, although it is not necessary to have a direct comparison between mechanically printed letters and handwritten ones, there are now several typefaces that have been designed to work on the same principle as handwriting.

Sassoon Primary was designed to look somewhat like handwriting. Exit strokes clump the words together to make them more easily readable. Line, word, and letter spacing can be varied to help problem readers.

'Sassoon Primary' is the typeface that provides a link between reading and writing. The exit strokes not only mean that the printed letters resemble written ones, but they have a function in clumping the words to accentuate the word shape. Different line, word and letter spacing is suggested for those with reading problems.

I couldn't face writing out seven years' worth of copy sheets, and designed a typeface of the model alphabet instead. Now the teachers can type in the text they want on a word processor, run it through a joiner program, and knock it out on a laserprinter.

A joined italic typeface to be used in conjunction with a handwriting scheme for Iceland, designed by G. SE Briem.

Explaining the change of attitude

If movement is to be the first priority then parents need to be informed, as well as nursery school teachers. As soon as children can write as much as their own names they need to be helped to form letters which move correctly. The letters in children's names are those that they write most often, so those will be the ones most quickly automated. If they are not corrected early on, they may prove to be the most difficult to alter.

There is one further point that needs explaining. Handwriting that moves well and is starting to join is seldom as conventionally neat as print script, although it may well be much more mature and efficient. Parents should be encouraged not to be critical of this difference. Neat print script all too often disguises movement faults and these can cause problems at a later stage. Once the letters move correctly and handwriting starts to flow easily, there should be many fewer setbacks. There should then be plenty of time to refine the developing handwriting, join it and speed it up.

A neat print may be useful in specific circumstances later on in life. Even so, it will be more legible if it moves correctly. The point that needs to be made is that print script is neither the only, nor the best early training for the efficient movement we need today.

4 The concepts behind our alphabet

Handwriting is a taught skill. It may seem a relatively simple task to an adult, but few of the ideas behind handwriting come naturally to children. Letters first probably appear to them as an unintelligible pattern of strokes, so when children first start to copy letters they see them as a visual pattern or shape. Learning to recognise the separate shapes of letters is sufficiently difficult for a young child, but our alphabet works as a moving pattern, so children then have to learn that strokes must move in a specific way. This is just one of the concepts, though perhaps the most difficult, that have to be learned.

The rules that govern handwriting vary from culture to culture, and many of these rules entail difficult perceptual or motor tasks for young children. There are so many things that have to come together before a young child can write or even copy a word. It is therefore essential that those of us who teach children how to write are aware of the concepts that govern our writing system. Briefly they are as follows:

1. The direction of writing is from left to right, and from the top of the page downwards.

2. Each letter has a correct movement, so the strokes that make up each letter must commence at the appropriate point and proceed in the correct direction.

3. Letters have specific height differentials.

4. Several sets of letters are mirror images of each other; these may need extra care in the teaching.

5. Capital letters and small letters have different uses.

6. Handwriting requires consistent letter spacing and adequate word spacing.

Once these separate ideas are understood, teachers will be in a better position to pass them on to their pupils. Exactly how these ideas are taught must be left to individuals, but children will need to have learned and practised most of them, either in pattern or some other form, before they are ready to copy whole words.

These concepts provide the basis of how to teach handwriting so they deserve to be looked at in more detail.

The direction of writing

This is a particular problem for left-handers so they may need more tracing or tracking practice, preferably at the pre-writing stage, to reinforce the correct direction. This must be supervised just as carefully as actual letters otherwise all that may happen is that the incorrect (right to left) direction may be reinforced. Without this help some left-handers may start writing at the wrong end of the line. Whichever hand is used, this is likely to result in mirror writing, where letters appear not only reversed but in reverse order. Mirror writing, therefore, could be described not so much as a sign of anything wrong with the pupil, but of a deficiency in the early teaching method.

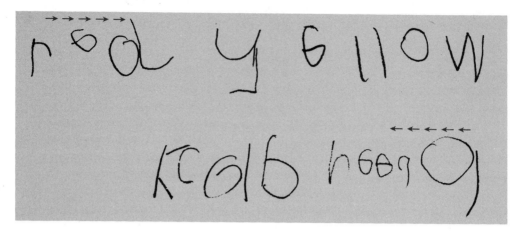

Handwriting is a taught skill; nothing is 'natural'. This child turns back from right to left at the end of the line. The Greeks called this 'boustrophedon' – the way the ploughing ox turns.

The movement of letters

The importance of correct movement is not always immediately apparent. It is usually possible to decipher young children's early attempts at large separate letters whether they move correctly or not. The real problems arise later when writing gets smaller, faster and more personal. Our alphabet has been designed to use only a few distinctive strokes so that any distortion can mean that it becomes difficult to discriminate between letters. An incorrect movement is likely to affect legibility more readily in joined letters, but separate letters with an incorrect movement also deteriorate at speed. This often happens when unusual movements of the hand exert pressures that distort the written strokes.

It is essential that the correct movement of the basic letters should be taught to young children as soon as they start school. This is most easily done by dividing letters into stroke-related families, not teaching the letters alphabetically. Any letters that children already write with an incorrect movement must be corrected straight away because the longer they are left the more difficult they are to alter.

The strokes of basic letters must start at the correct point and move in the right direction. Retraining is not easy once a wrong movement has become automatic.

Height differentials

This important aspect of our alphabet determines the shape of words and affects the legibility of handwriting. Children need help initially to understand the relative heights of individual letters such as 'i', 'l' and 't' ('t' is a mid-height letter), and that some letters descend below the baseline. A baseline, double lines or even four lines may be needed to explain or practise the different heights of letters which can be a considerable problem for some young children. When older pupils allow the height differentials of their letters to become eroded their handwriting, however 'neat', may be difficult to decipher. At this (or any other) time reinforcement of this rule may be needed.

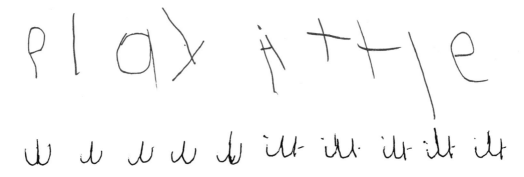

Differentiating between the heights of letters is a major problem for young children. Subtler points can still trouble much older pupils.

Mirror images

This is a slightly different issue and arises because several pairs of letters in our alphabet are mirror images of each other. This is once again the result of an alphabet that uses such a limited number of strokes. Young children may not have developed the visual discrimination to recognise the differences, so 'b' and 'd', or 'p' and 'q' may present special problems. If teachers can be aware of this at the pre-writing stage then simple sorting, matching or pattern tasks can be devised to prepare young children for discriminating between mirror images.

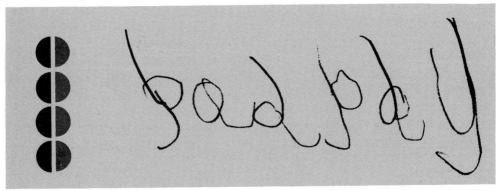

A case of mirror-image confusion. This difficult discrimination might be easier for young children if they were exposed to it in play and pattern situations before starting to write.

Ben ING now de

My name smith hnhn

Ben's problem arose from the movement of the 'N' in his name, carried through to 'n', and then being told 'h' is a tall 'n'. Differences in movement between 'M-m' and 'N-n' can confuse.

Capital letters

The difference between capital letters and small letters needs to be explained to children. Many parents still teach capital letters to their children in the belief that they are easier, so reception teachers need a convincing explanation. Capital letters have clear uses in our writing system, so children's names can be used to show that only the first letter should be a capital. Teachers themselves may be unaware of the origin of the different letters. A somewhat simplistic historical explanation is often useful for older pupils. Capital letters were most often used in inscriptions because they consist mostly of straight lines which are easy to cut. As too many straight strokes and angular changes of direction would slow down handwriting, small letters developed with curved strokes that could flow easily. We still keep capital letters for the important initials in names, to mark the start of a sentence and to stress headings.

Spacing

Letter spacing seems less of a conceptual problem for young children than word spacing, although it may be difficult in practice. The spacing between words needs careful explanation. It is important therefore, that teachers themselves first have a clear understanding of the issue. The space between words needs to be related to the size of the letters, so children can be told to leave the space of one letter. Perhaps the letter 'o' is the most appropriate. Typographers have long used this way of word spacing. In schools, however, the idea of finger or thumb spacing is often used. Most children use this as a temporary aid and then discard it, but there are always a few who retain this concept of spacing into later school life. They then report that their huge word spaces are 'mental' finger spacing long after fingers have grown and writing has shrunk. Incidentally, word spacing is relatively recent; there were no spaces between words in classical Latin.

The history of the development of our alphabet is not only a fascinating study but often useful for those who need to understand the concepts that govern it. For instance, the dot on the letter 'i', which hardly merits being a separate concept, arose out of necessity at a certain stage in history when the Gothic 'textura' letters were popular. It became impossible to tell the difference between such letters or combinations as 'in' and 'm' without a distinguishing mark over the 'i'. We still need it for more or less the same reason.

kee P th qt   Keepothat

The space between words should be approximately the size of an 'o', not the size of a thumb.

Teaching the concepts behind our alphabet

Once the importance of these concepts is recognised, then they can be taught imaginatively and with confidence. Simple terminology can be chosen to explain them to the youngest children. This way of tackling the very basics of writing is at variance with what at present goes on in many infant schools. Far too often young children are set to trace or copy a message from the board such as 'my first day at school', to take home to eager parents. It would be in the children's best interest to introduce each of the concepts separately, with a careful oral explanation. They can then be practised one at a time, through pattern, letter-pattern, kinaesthetically or by any other appropriate method. Ideally all this should happen before young children set about trying to copy whole words.

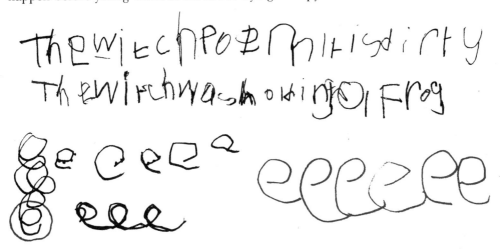

Some children fail to learn by the same method as others, either visually or kinaesthetically. This boy could not produce a conventional letter 'e' from the usual patterns, only when the movement was explained: 'start from the middle and go up and round'.

Spacing and the letter 'e' improved after explicit instruction, but there was still a lot to do.

The purpose of handwriting

Although it is essential, in the early stages, to separate lessons in the skill of handwriting from those concerned with creative writing, children need to understand the purpose of what they are doing. To a young child, letters are just a pattern of strokes, and they may be adept at copying such a pattern without understanding that it has any real meaning. We allot sounds to the patterns of strokes that make up individual letters and we then group letters together in a more complex pattern, to represent a word. This may be so obvious to adults that they do not realise how confusing it may be for the few children who proudly produce an accurate pattern one day and are praised for it, but are criticised for a slightly different one another day. No child will suffer from listening to a short explanation of the purpose of letters, but a few will be confused without it.

5 How you write in terms of posture is as important as what you write in terms of letters

'Handwriting posture' is a term that includes not only how writers sit but how they use their arms and hold their pens. These three factors are usually interdependent. Moreover, they can all be affected by where the writer positions the paper on the desk. Postural habits soon become automated just like the movement of letters. The hand, indeed the whole body needs to be well positioned so that it can function at its best for writing. Good posture needs to be learned from the beginning so that later in life the hand can work freely and without pain, to produce a fast, legible handwriting.

The factors that may influence posture

The idea that 'how you write in terms of posture is as important as what you write, and inevitably affects your letters', should be introduced at the very start of children's school life. Once the importance of postural factors is recognised, the decision concerning how to introduce it to a classroom of young children must lie with individual schools. There are many practical factors to consider and not all of them are the sole responsibility of the reception teacher.

This left-hander's inverted penhold and stiff fingers pushed the pen in a clockwise movement. The resulting backward loops caused awkward arm movements and illegible handwriting.

Appropriate furniture

Not all children are the same size at the same age. Furniture that is either too large or too small can prevent children from sitting properly. A variety of furniture may be desirable in classrooms, even if this looks untidy or causes organisational difficulties. In ideal circumstances, children should be encouraged to report if they are not comfortable when sitting down to write. A sloped writing surface encourages good writing posture, but desks with sloping tops are seldom found in schools today, although freely available for designers or architects. They disappeared from classrooms when teaching methods altered and are unlikely to reappear, although it is always possible that separate writing boards could be made available when handwriting is being taught. The idea that sloping surfaces are beneficial, has been ignored for so long that even in therapy departments, where adjustable tables are usually available, they are seldom used when helping children (or adults) with handwriting problems.

When several secondary schools were surveyed on the subject of comfort and furniture, many pupils reported to the teachers concerned that although they had known that they were not comfortable they had not bothered to say anything as they did not think anything would be done about it.

Being too tall for junior school desks meant that this girl got used to sitting sideways. She did not alter her posture and eventually, at fifteen, the way in which she sat resulted in such pain that she almost stopped writing altogether. Changing her posture and penhold cured the pain but not before she had fallen behind in her work.

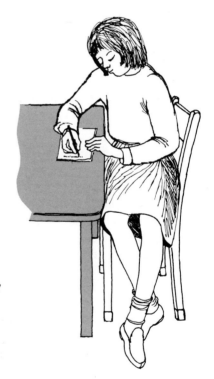

The pains in my hand have completely vanished

Paper position and size

The way that writers choose to place their paper on the desk often determines their posture. The action of placing the paper in the same position each time becomes so automatic that writers seldom recognise this as a likely cause of bad posture or discomfort when writing. An informed attitude is needed to help children find an appropriate paper position. It is usually best for right-handers to place their paper to their right side and left-handers to their left, so the writing hand can move freely and the line of vision is clear. The writer can then tilt the paper to a comfortable angle. There cannot and should not be a rigid ruling about paper position because so many personal differences need to be considered. For example, sometimes the eyes must be considered as well as the hand, or even the back in the case of certain disabilities. Placing the paper in a position that permits the writer to develop good writing posture, presupposes that there is always room in the classroom, at a desk or a table, for each child to adopt an appropriate paper position.

Matters such as paper size also need to be taken into consideration if the suggestion of an optimum writing position is to be carried to its logical conclusion. Sheets that are too large may mean children having to stretch in an awkward way to reach the top. It is better to have smaller sheets and introduce children to the idea that paper should be moved to a convenient position rather than the body be distorted to accommodate the paper.

One seven-year-old boy proudly showed his school-made, scrap-book-sized handwriting book. When asked how he managed to reach the top lines where the text was written (the bottom half was reserved for illustrations), he described how 'of course' the chairs were too low to let him reach, so he lay flat on the table to write.

A choice of pens and pencils

It is a good idea to provide a variety of pencils of different shapes and sizes, or pens at a later stage, as well as some with different kinds of points. Children appear to have distinct preferences for a certain size, shape or even 'feel' of pencils from an early age. What suits one child's hand may not suit another, but the children themselves are seldom consulted, so-called experts too often making decisions on their behalf. For many years, it has been the custom to recommend extra fat pencils for young children to write with. Observant teachers notice that a few children, given the choice, may choose fat ones but the majority choose ordinary-sized ones. With pens the point is as important as the barrel. Left-handers, in particular, need soft leads and points that move smoothly across the page. The pen and pencil preference surveys in Part 2 of this book provide ample evidence of children's views on this subject.

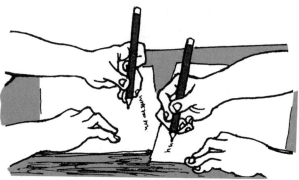

A right-hander and a left-hander show different ways of holding felt-tipped pens in an upright position in which they work best.

Penhold

The whole position of penhold is complicated by the use of modern pens – felt-tipped perhaps for the younger children and fibre-tipped or ballpoint for the older ones. Most modern pens work at a different elevation to traditional fountain pens or pencils. While the teaching profession is still committed to encouraging children to use the conventional tripod grip, more and more pupils seem to be adopting unconventional penholds. This may be an attempt on the part of children to develop their own strategies for using modern pens. An unconventional penhold may be successful for a particular writer despite appearing to the teacher to be uncomfortable. There is an alternative penhold that seems to work well for all kinds of pens, and it is often adopted spontaneously by young children as well as older people who find it relaxing and efficient. It seems to be suitable for those with long fingers who often experience pain when writing at speed with a conventional penhold. However, it is not advisable to recommend this for universal use without much more research. Until then, all those concerned with handwriting need to become aware of the problems of penhold, and with increasing experience, learn to help individuals find something that suits them, both in terms of pen and penhold.

This pupil had found for herself that the alternative penhold worked well. She had resisted pressure to change, from both school and home and her writing was excellent.

Left-handers' special needs

Left-handers may need different conditions and different strategies from right-handers. As the direction of their writing moves towards their bodies they may, amongst other problems, have difficulty seeing what they have just written. Poor spacing is often an indication that children cannot see what they have just written. Some left-handers may signal their special needs by adopting such strategies as inverted hand positions, where the hand is twisted so the pen writes from above the line. However, if they are given consideration and suitable strategies are taught from the start, left-handers might have fewer problems. It has already been explained how important it is for left-handers to place their paper to their left side so that they can see what they are writing. It can also help if their chair is slightly higher than usual so that the writers can see over their hand. Needless to say, a chair that is too low will be an added disadvantage to left-handers. They may also need to be encouraged not to hold the pencil too near the point as this is another way of interrupting the line of vision. However, it is only the thumb that gets in the way, so do not be surprised when left-handers find ways of tucking it out of the way. This may look unusual but it works. The alternative penhold also works well for left-handers

The importance of good light

Another often forgotten factor that contributes to vision and posture is light. All writers need good light in order to sit up straight and still see what they are doing. (This pre-supposes that all pupils have good eyesight or have had their eyes tested for the many problems that might be affecting their ability to retain conventionally good posture.) The lighting in rooms is sometimes arranged so that it is only good for right-handers, in which case left-handers will be writing in the shadow of their own hand. This can result in children hunched over their work in order to see what they are doing, a habit that once established is hard to break. (See page 95 for more details on posture.)

Lines and their effect on the size of letters and possibly on writing posture

Schools may have definite views on the use of either plain or lined paper at different ages. Some have rigid attitudes, forbidding any lines in infant schools, while others prescribe sets of lines of specific spacing for each age group from school entry. Where surveys have been carried out (by teachers on in-service courses), it has been shown that those young children who manage best without lines find most difficulty in adhering to them later on, and those who have encountered problems managing without lines find them a positive and immediate advantage when they are allowed to use lined paper. This alone would point to the need for a more flexible attitude, but there are other aspects to consider. Judging the different height of letters is a difficult task for young children. A baseline, at least, may be needed to help children understand how some letters have descending strokes and other ascenders. Many children might benefit temporarily from two, three or even four lines to help them come to terms with the height differentials of letters. This does not mean that they need such lines all the time. For this purpose different-sized, staved training lines can be useful.

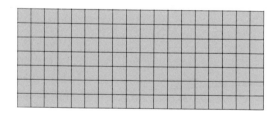

Squared paper helps alignment without imposing size.

Staved lines help young children, but several sizes may be needed.

Whatever a particular school's view, at some stage lines are introduced and they begin to influence the size of pupils' handwriting. This will have even more impact if double lines are used. It is now beginning to be understood not only that some children prefer to write somewhat larger or smaller than their peers, but also that changes in size may affect their actual writing strategies. If a child is asked to write very large or very small, and then in other sizes in between, it will become evident to an observant watcher that alterations occur in several aspects of handwriting posture. The hand and sometimes the whole arm works differently depending on the size of the writing. The head position may change as writing gets smaller, and the whole way of sitting too. If children are asked which size they find easiest to write in and which size they have to write in at school, the answers are seldom the same. This points to the suggestion that there should be a flexible attitude to the size of writing and a choice of lines, rather than imposing or even expecting one size to be appropriate for all hands and for all children of the same age. In this way, the few problem children who really need to find a posture to suit themselves will not be penalised by too rigid an attitude to size. The squared paper that is used in many European countries can be beneficial in the early stages of handwriting, giving a certain amount of help in alignment without imposing either a slant or a size.

The position of the hand may affect the slant of the handwriting. When the hand is on edge, providing that it is relaxed, the writing may slant forward. When the hand is slightly flattened, the writing may be more upright.

Slant and proportion of letters

It is not widely realised that the slant and proportion of letters are influenced to a considerable extent by how writers use their hands. These two aspects of letters may assume importance where a school imposes a strict model. The position of the hand, whether it is on edge, slightly on edge or flattened is likely to influence the slant of letters. The way the fingers are positioned on the pen, in particular the one which is nearest the point and therefore exerts most lateral pressure, can affect the proportion of letters. In terms of writing posture, this means that many children cannot follow the school's model because the way they use their hands precludes the slant or proportion of the letters. It means that they are having to fight against the way their hand or arm works most easily, and in extreme cases children find such difficulty in reproducing a model that does not come naturally to them, that they do not manage to automate the act of handwriting. The way the hand and finger positions affect letters needs to be explained to older pupils, and once it is understood by those who plan policies, their attitude to rigid models might be modified.

Conclusions

Previously, some of these factors may not have been considered to affect posture, but by looking at them in a slightly different way, they can now be shown to be important. If children are to write freely it must be in a way that works for their whole body. This is why it is also necessary to be relaxed in order to write well. Of course it may not always be possible to ensure that a writer is relaxed; life both inside and outside school may be full of frustrations and worries. Extreme tension, however, can so distort posture that it interrupts the free movement of the hand and arm, so teachers must always be aware of this possibility. A tense writer may produce tense, even ugly-looking letters. This needs to be calmly recognised without criticism, as criticism can only lead to further physical tension and possibly worse writing. Positive help in the way of exercises may sometimes be needed to help those in trouble to relax and to regain a more comfortable writing posture. Increasing tension coupled with almost any of the aspects of poor writing posture can lead to pain. Pain is the body's warning system, which when ignored, can lead to the serious condition known as writer's cramp.

The kind of questions that teachers should be asking their pupils, depending on their age are:

1. Can you sit comfortably on your chair to write at your desk?

2. Can you see what you are writing?

3. Have you got enough space in which to place your paper in the best position for you to write?

4. Can you move your arm freely when writing?

5. Do you like the pen or pencil that you are using?

6. Do the lines on the paper suit the size of your writing?

7. Does the way you hold your pen allow you to write as fast as you need to?

8. Do you find it a problem to keep to the slant or proportions of the letters in the school model or, for that matter to be consistent in any particular slant?

9. Are you aware of being tense? If you are, do you know how to relax your hand or arm?

10. Does your hand, arm or neck ache when you write for any length of time?

6 A systematic teaching method is needed – not necessarily a strict model

I want to focus here on the need for a systematic teaching method that would ensure that all young children are exposed to, and then practised in, each formative stage of basic handwriting.

Practised writers perform each of the separate actions that are involved in the act of 'writing' so automatically, that it is not easy to separate all these tasks in order to understand how to teach them. Once the complex sequence is worked out, a consistent attitude is needed throughout schools to ensure that there is a smooth progression towards a fast efficient handwriting, from school entry to school leaving. Imagination and a certain flexibility are both needed within any system, and maybe these are the difficult areas to work out.

The suggestions set out here are equally relevant to those countries who already provide a structured handwriting curriculum, and to those like Great Britain, where choice of such matters as model and details of method are left to individual schools. Some regional or national policies provide sensible age-related targets which relate to children's actual needs in the classroom. Other curriculum documents may include adequate instructions on the more practical issues of handwriting, but frequently both teachers and inspectors judge the success or failure of a policy by the degree of adherence to the latest model. Meanwhile in other places and according to other 'experts', it is deemed not necessary to teach the skill of handwriting at all and it is suggested that skill training, or emphasis on 'correct' letters, is likely to repress the creativity of content in children's early written work.

The real need must be somewhere in between these two. Pupils need an adequate handwriting that can record their thoughts at a reasonable speed, otherwise there will be a permanent curb on their creativity. A structure is needed to ensure that those aspects of handwriting that are essential should be taught thoroughly and systematically particularly at the vital early stages. A model may well be helpful to the teacher in the early stages but it should primarily be used to stress the movement of letters. However once children are competent and confirmed in the correct movement of letters they should be encouraged to progress to a fast legible handwritng unhampered by the need to conform to a strict model that might be personally inappropriate. Some joins should develop spontaneously if the suggestions on page 9 about teaching letters with an exit stroke are followed. Other types of joins will need to be taught. At this stage pupils can be encouraged to speed up their writing. The best advice to give them may be to join letters when they feel comfortable about it but to be free to take a penlift as desired, with no sense of obligation to join every letter all the time. Few adults write more than four or five letters at a time without taking a penlift. As each of the issues concerning handwriting is discussed, it becomes more obvious that here is a subject that perhaps cannot be measured in terms of norms or averages. It is individual attainment within a structured, yet flexible system that is really important.

A flexible system

Any system should be flexible enough to work for those who, for whatever reason, are likely to have difficulty in learning to write, as well as for those who are likely to have little difficulty in acquiring a flowing hand. The purpose of a systematic method should be that the stages can be subdivided and taught more slowly and repetitively for those who find writing difficult, but always with the same goals in mind. In this way there should be a progression towards each individual's optimum.

The personal nature of handwriting can never be ignored from either the perspective of the teacher or the pupil. It is almost impossible to measure such matters as the quality of handwriting, much less the more complex matter of legibility. What one person might praise as good, clear handwriting, another might dislike for its immaturity or for subjective, aesthetic reasons. What one person finds 'illegible' may be quite legible to another. Those accustomed to teaching the youngest age groups may find it difficult to understand that there are many acceptable and perfectly legible variations on the basic letterforms taught in infant schools. In a mature adult hand these variations are quite acceptable and legible to the reader; in pupils' handwriting they are all too often criticised, instead of being recognised as a sign of maturity.

It is not always easy to differentiate between those variations that disrupt an efficient movement or that are likely to produce an unrecognisable ligature, and personal variations that may lead to a more efficient form within a writer's personal style. This, however, is the guidance that our pupils need if they are to develop their handwriting to the required level of legibility, at the speeds that they need today. This situation seems to call for more thorough training of teachers than was considered necessary before.

Small personal movements make handwriting interesting. Examples of variations in the movement of the letters 'th' in the word 'the' from children's handwriting, from Sassoon, Wing and Nimmo-Smith (1989, see page 36).

slow				
the	the	the	one	the
fast				
the	the	the	ore	the

Right-handers show how speed helps develop efficient joins.

the the	the the	the	ter	the
th	th	th	te	tt

Left-handers' solutions to crossbar joins.

24

7 Suggestions for curriculum planning

The propositions that have been put forward in the first part of this book have certain practical implications for our future curriculum planning. Handwriting should, and could, be relatively easy to teach, but unfortunately teachers are seldom trained to understand the importance of the early stages, or of a systematic method. The first battle must be to improve initial and in-service training, and then to try to remove some of the misconceptions that have arisen over the last few decades. When considering a handwriting policy, it is important to get the priorities right, both in terms of other essential, related subjects and within the skill training of handwriting. The word 'priority' is used here in three ways:

1. The priority given to the skill of handwriting in the general curriculum

2. The priorities in the vital initial stages of learning

3. The changing priorities for the task as pupils grow older.

Overall priorities

The importance of a systematic method of skill training
The skill of handwriting needs to be taught separately from creative writing and it should not be confused with the letter-recognition aspect of reading. A systematic teaching method is needed that emphasises the importance of the correct movement of basic letters. If adequate time and resources are concentrated on in the first vital year, the long remedial struggle and the problems that arise from not having an adequate handwriting can be minimised.

However good the teaching there will always be some children with real difficulties. A systematic method should not only profit the majority who learn easily but also benefit those who might find writing difficult. The stages of the handwriting system can be subdivided into smaller and more repetitive steps for those who are less competent than others in the early stages. Such a system soon shows up those with more severe problems. An early diagnosis will enable them to receive the extra help that will prevent them falling too far behind the rest of the class.

Good handwriting posture is essential for efficient handwriting
Good posture and habits help to promote good handwriting at any age. Practical matters should be considered as much a part of any handwriting policy as the letters themselves. These factors include appropriate-sized furniture so that large and small pupils are equally comfortable, guidance with paper position for both left- and right-handers and an understanding of penhold. A flexible attitude towards materials such as pens and pencils, and lined or unlined paper would ensure that pupils find what is best suited to their personal needs. All these factors help the writing hand to function at its best, and allow the pen to move in a controlled but relaxed way.

It is the movement of letters that matters most

Handwriting must first of all be legible and then be fast enough to do its job. The correct movement of letters is necessary to produce legible writing, and an efficient movement is needed to enable it to speed up. This movement should not have to change from reception class to maturity. Movement must not be confused with shape or style. Handwriting is such a personal matter that there is always a risk that by imposing a formal model and demanding a specific slant or proportion of letter, some children will be disadvantaged. A policy should take into consideration from the start that writers are individuals and that certain aspects of handwriting are individual too. A good overall policy should reflect the needs of the writers, allow for differing written tasks, and be flexible enough to work with and for different people.

Changing priorities throughout school life

Priority at pre-school stage (c. 3–5); preparing for the task of writing

Children are often insufficiently prepared for the complex task of writing that faces them at school entry. They need graphic experience and specific activities that teach hand/eye co-ordination and visual discrimination. They need the vocabulary to comprehend the teaching of direction and other essential concepts. They will benefit from exercises that help them to understand the concepts that rule our alphabet: direction of writing and stroke, height differential and mirror image. In addition, social training is needed to prepare them to sit still and concentrate, even for a short time, on a precision task, and to give them the confidence to approach handwriting in a relaxed way.

Priorities for infants (c. 5–7); getting off to the best possible start

What is learned at school entry is going to influence children's handwriting habits for many years. The key issues are:

1. When to start

2. How to start

3. What letters to teach.

When to start   Some children may not be ready to learn to write when they enter school at the age of five, as in Great Britain, or six, as in many other countries. Other children may have already learned a certain amount at home or in a pre-school group. Some instruction must be given to children once they are in a formal teaching situation otherwise, by uncontrolled experiment, they may develop just the habits that are so difficult to correct. Those who have already learned to write letters with an incorrect movement will need remedial help as soon as possible.

It is also just as harmful to hold back children who are ready to write as it is to push those who are not ready. Inevitably, there will have to be a certain amount of grouping of children if there are marked differences in their graphic development. Extra emphasis may be needed on pre-writing skills where necessary.

How to start   Initial emphasis must be on the correct point of entry and direction of the strokes of basic letters. The letters are most easily learned when taught in stroke-related families rather than alphabetically. In this way, teachers can ensure that the correct movement of each group of letters has been assimilated before introducing the next.

What letters to teach   Letters with exit strokes at the baseline encourage a relaxed movement that soon leads to spontaneous baseline joins. The exit strokes also promote natural spacing of letters. This avoids the poor spacing often evident in teenage print script where letters are superimposed on each other. Exit strokes lead to a flowing movement between letters, whether this movement is visible on the paper as in joined letters, or in the air as a consequence of a penlift.

Priorities for lower juniors (c. 7–9); when, how and why to teach joins

If any pupils are writing any of their basic letters with an incorrect movement, then this must be corrected before encouraging any joins at all. Exit strokes should have promoted the right movement for baseline joins, then crossbar and other joins need to be taught in their respective groups. Children should be encouraged to join letters when they feel comfortable rather than every letter all the time. This promotes a fast, efficient writing that allows the hand to move freely along the line.

Priorities for top juniors (c. 9–11); refining joins and speeding up

Pupils need to be confirmed in their joins before they leave junior school. They need help in speeding up their writing and an explanation of the different levels of writing required for different tasks. It is only fair to explain that there is a balance between speed and legibility. Guided experiments with a variety of writing implements can help pupils to discover the pen that best suits both their hand and their handwriting. Informed teachers could advise on which personal variations of letterforms are desirable, in that they increase the efficiency of the handwriting, and which ones might deteriorate and affect legibility. It is often the last time for sorting out any problems. Secondary schools expect pupils to be able to write adequately and seldom have time or facilities for dealing with the teaching of handwriting.

Priorities for secondary entrance (11+); reassessment – new school, new needs

Many children enter secondary school not only with inadequate handwriting, but also with no idea of the differing needs of tasks like note taking. All pupils would benefit from an explanation of the expectations of the written tasks in their new curriculum. At this stage an assessment of problems might also be useful. This can be done by individual testing or in groups. Another way would be encourage those who feel that they need help to ask for it. Pupils with severe problems are going to need extra attention if they are not to become increasingly handicapped by poor handwriting. This should not be confused with other remedial teaching; high achievers often have difficulty with handwriting.

Priorities for mid-secondary (13+); experimentation and personal solutions

This is a time for experimentation (with or without the participation of teachers). The effects of any previous model will have been diluted by now and teenagers will be searching not only for a writing that expresses their individuality but one that works for them. Their handwriting therefore may vary from page to page, and peer group idiosyncrasies may test the tolerance of the teacher. However, the development of a personal hand will continue as the pupil matures. Understanding appraisal on the part of any teacher (not only the English staff) will help pupils to acquire the fast, personal movement that in the end is the soundest basis for an efficient, consistent hand. It is at this stage, more than perhaps at any other, that uninformed criticism is counter-productive. A careful diagnosis is needed if there is a problem, followed by an explanation and constructive suggestions.

Priorities for top secondary (15+); preparing for the stress of exams

Another assessment of pupils' needs might be a good idea now. Those starting on external examinations may need help as they attempt to write even faster without sacrificing legibility. They may also need practical help in controlling the effects of stress. This could include tips on relaxing tense penholds. Those intending to leave school need a different kind of help: how to fill in forms neatly and legibly, how to make the best of their handwriting in terms of maturity and presentation, and perhaps stage-by-stage guidance on drafting letters of application. These factors could make a difference to their job prospects.

Top priority at any age

If a pupil has handwriting problems, the following are essential:

1. An accurate diagnosis

2. An explanation

3. Practical suggestions for a remedy

4. Plenty of encouragement.

8 The case for a consistent terminology

A detailed and consistent terminology is essential to enable people to communicate on the subject of handwriting; it is just as necessary to help individuals reach a precise understanding of what they are observing.

When a collection of people discuss handwriting specific terms need defining, otherwise purposeless arguments and needless misunderstandings can arise just because people use different terminologies.

There are alternative names for many of the specific forms of letters that it is necessary to describe. These need defining to avoid unnecessary misunderstandings. In other cases, there is no term specific enough to describe some quite common features of handwriting. Some new terms are needed so that these features can be observed precisely, and the implications can be discussed.

The word 'writing' itself has several meanings, more often being thought of as describing content rather than the act of writing. This use of one word for several purposes may have contributed to the neglect of the specific skill aspect of (hand)writing that concerns this book. The confusion continues when terms such as 'bad' or 'untidy' are related to a page of writing. These terms often refer more to presentation than to the letters concerned. Presentation is important, and children need to be taught how to lay their work out, but it is a slightly different issue.

The terminology of the subject of handwriting has a nasty habit of varying from one profession to another. This is likely to create more difficulties in a subject where teachers, psychologists, letterform specialists and perhaps palaeographers or forensic document examiners need to understand each other. Forensic experts may seem an unlikely group to mention, but they have produced some of the research that is most relevant to this book. Their job is to catch forgers, so they are well aware of the variations of letterforms, and the characteristics that people find either easy or particularly difficult to change. The terms that are used throughout this book to describe different aspects of letterforms are described in this section to help clear up some of the areas of confusion. I have stopped short of producing a glossary of terms because, however desirable it might be to have a common terminology that could apply to the many disciplines involved in letterforms, in practice there are still considerable problems and prejudices to overcome. It will be many years before printers stop using their cherished 'upper and lower case' to describe capital and small letters, which are now the recommended terms.

Parts of letters

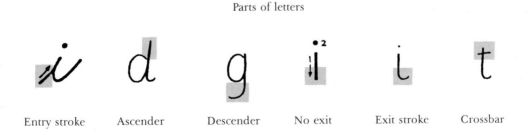

| Entry stroke | Ascender | Descender | No exit | Exit stroke | Crossbar |

Parts of letters

Terms such as 'entry stroke' and 'exit stroke' will become obvious as this book proceeds. The different elements of letters are illustrated on pages 29 and 55. It is important that all of these possibly unfamiliar details are understood by teachers. Once the meaning is clear they are then free to choose the terminology to use in class. The children themselves have a way of inventing explicit terms for exit strokes and other parts of letters for instance, but everyone (and that means the children as well as other teachers) needs to understand exactly what is meant by any particular term. Even the simplest words such as 'up' or 'down' can be ambiguous. When teachers write on the board what is often called an 'up' or a 'down' stroke it does not mean the same in directional terms for children who are writing at a table. For them the same strokes are not 'up' or 'down', but movements towards or away from the body.

Capital letters and small letters

The terms 'separate letters' and 'joined letters' are quite clear and need no further definition, but there can be different kinds of separate letters. It is possible to describe capital letters as separate. Everyone knows what capital letters are, although some people might call them majuscules, derived from Latin, or upper case after the outdated way that typesetters used to store capital letters in a wooden case above the other letters that became known in the trade as 'lower case'. How do you explain that to a five-year-old?

The letters which are not capitals can then be called lower case or minuscules but it would be far better to use a term such as 'small letters' that could be easily understood by all of those whose work involves dealing with letters. We need simple terms that can cross multi-disciplinary boundaries.

Teacher:	*'I use the terms capital letters and lower case, because when I tell the children to use 'small' letters they just reduce the size.'*
Answer:	*'If you feel strongly about this issue then why not drop the word 'case'. This is the illogical part of the term because it refers to the box in which the letters were stored. Then you could use the terms capital letters and lower letters. At least both those terms would be relevant to children's handwriting, but teachers have been referring to big 'A' little 'a' for centuries with no trouble.'*

Print and print script

Small letters themselves can be of different kinds and these also need careful description. The word 'print' often refers to typographic letters of all kinds that are printed by machine. Print has also come to mean a simple letter, sometimes a capital letter, to be used when filling out forms.

The term 'print script' as used in Great Britain describes a written 'small letter' that teachers describe as 'looking like the type in children's reading books' (which of course it often does not). A more precise description would be to use the typographic descriptor 'sanserif', which translated into handwriting terms, means a simplified letter with no entry strokes or exit strokes (except occasionally 't'). It is these downstrokes without terminal strokes that differentiate print script letters from any other small separate letter. Some representations of print script show a little movement within letters, others demonstrate a distinct penlift between the strokes. The term 'ball and stick writing' is sometimes used instead of print script in Great Britain but more often in other countries. The name suggests the stiffness of the letterforms, but the term is not always understood or used accurately. To add to the confusion, what the British call print script is sometimes called manuscript in other countries.

Occasionally the term 'print script' is used to describe letters that have exit strokes but this is not strictly accurate. The specific but rather lengthy term 'separate letters with exit strokes' is used in this book to describe the letterforms recommended for teaching to young children. The terms 'flowing separate letters' and 'flow letters' mean the same, and are other terms that have been used to describe letters with exit strokes. No doubt other similar words will appear as these letters replace traditional print script.

Cursive or semi-cursive

The terms that refer to the joining of letters need to be clarified. Two letters are clearly joined or unjoined, or are they? Two letters that touch may look as if they join but in handwriting terms there is a difference between those that merely touch and those that join without a penlift. That gives three descriptors of letters in relation to each other, but they are seldom sufficient to describe the letters of a long word, much less a page or even a line of writing. Adults seldom join all their letters together all the time. They take a penlift after every few letters to let the hand move along the line. There is no word to describe this ordinary, variable handwriting where the letters sometimes join and sometimes do not. The word 'cursive' is often used to describe handwriting; it comes from the Latin word meaning running. Ask a roomful of people what the word cursive means to them and it is likely that their answers will vary considerably. Does cursive mean that every letter is always joined or just some? It may sound trivial but it is really very important in the context of handwriting policy. There is a need for at least two distinct terms, 'continuous cursive' and 'semi-cursive'. Continuous cursive would describe only those models or examples of handwriting where all the letters within a word are joined all the time. This would include looped descenders. Semi-cursive would still be rather a broad term describing handwriting where some but not all letters joined. A more specific description such as 'simplified cursive' might be needed for models of handwriting such as the one Marion Richardson prescribed. In her model, the simplified letters 'b' and 'p' promoted joins that made joining easier for young children. She never advocated joins from descending strokes so, as long as the teachers understood this, children using Marion Richardson books were (and still are) not brought up to join every letter all the time. These three terms for joined or cursive letters, 'continuous', 'semi' and 'simplified' would allow the important differences between the concepts and resulting handwriting to be understood. They would make it possible to describe more accurately the kind of handwriting that children need to learn.

Model, style and method

There is another group of terms that are often misused: 'model', 'style' and 'method'. They need defining, or perhaps separating. The word 'model' should mean the letterforms that are to be copied in a generic sense. The word 'style' could be defined as the writer's (or perhaps teacher's) particular interpretation of the model. It suggests a more personal element and is a less formal word. The 'method' of writing is how someone chooses to write. It can include the practical aspects of handwriting like penhold and paper position. It can also refer to the writing implement, the desk angle and even the preferred type of paper for writing. Recommended methods of writing can vary considerably in any of these elements.

Models and methods are distinct concepts and this needs to be appreciated particularly for planning purposes. Model and method can in certain circumstances contain elements that are dependent on each other. The model may include those elements of method considered essential for its reproduction, for instance the use of a broad-edge nib for italic writing, although this does not mean that italic cannot be produced with another type of pen. A method may also include a specific model, but in spite of this, both model and method can be independently described. Incorrect or uninformed terminology creates confusion, but a precise terminology can lead the way to an understanding of some of the less familiar but important concepts behind the teaching of handwriting.

Movement of letters

The idea that handwriting should be considered in terms of movement instead of as immobile black marks on a page, needs clarifying. If letters are to be considered in relation to the hand that writes them, then a single stroke of the pen is not just a mark on the paper but the trace of a movement. A single line can be described as a movement in one direction or another. The movement within letters can usually be described as involving a retrace where there is no penlift. The hand can move during the act of writing but leave no trace on the paper. This happens when the writer lifts the pen and repositions it. Penlifts can occur within or between letters, as well as between words. Joins can be described as the visible trace of the movement between letters. The actual movement of the hand can be recorded by special equipment. In the case of joins, this equipment can help assess the relative efficiency of perhaps joining two letters, or lifting and repositioning the pen while writing them. The combination of the visible trace of the movement of hand and pen, plus the invisible movement within or between letters, answers to the term 'ductus'. This term is often used by palaeographers who trace the changes in the movement of the letters of our alphabet (and others) as they constantly develop and alter over the centuries. This changing of the movement of letters is still going on, and the word 'ductus' is by no means redundant.

Once we are aware of such movements, it soon becomes possible to work out what actions the hand may be performing to produce any sequence of letters. In this way, an understanding of the terminology can lead to the observation of movement, and through that to a deeper comprehension of the complexities of handwriting.

PART 2

A new way of looking at handwriting

Handwriting is a complicated skill. If we want to understand what it is and how it works, we may find it best to divide the subject up and investigate the various aspects one by one. Eventually, all the factors need to be seen in relation to each other. My point is that only by observing and understanding the many interdependent features of handwriting will it be possible to plan an adequate curriculum, or intervene to help individuals with their problems. The level of knowledge about the subject is surprisingly low. Even at the research level few people have the knowledge, the time or the inclination to look at the different aspects of handwriting in relation to each other. Yet before any effective policy recommendations can be made we not only need to know details of all aspects of childrens' performance, but we need to be able to interpret the intricate web of findings in an informed and impartial way. My aim here is to suggest new strategies for looking at and understanding handwriting and to provide suggestions for carrying out simple research in the field that will make this possible.

9 The role of surveys and research

Extensive research projects and smaller school surveys can both be extremely valuable. They often provide much needed information to enable us to find out what is happening in our schools. In both cases if the complexity of writing is ignored, the resulting findings may not be relevant in a wider setting, but this does not mean that small surveys of certain separate aspects of handwriting are not useful. Observation of a small group of children can point the way to what is needed in specific circumstances, even if this is not sufficient to influence a regional or national policy. Surveying the different features of handwriting is just as important as it leads to an understanding of how it all works. On a more personal level, both surveys and research can be rewarding. However little time or money may be spent on it, any project involves delving deeper into the complexities of the chosen subject. The insight gained will lead to ever more informed observation. The benefits of such observations, however modest, will compound to make teachers or therapists more effective in their jobs – and often make everyday work more interesting as well.

Differences between surveys and research

It is my aim here to look at strategies for conducting surveys and research, and for using them as a tool for furthering our understanding of the act of writing. It is not easy to define the differences between a survey and a research project. Both require certain preliminary decisions to be made, such as what precisely to observe and how to go about this task. It is really a matter of depth and time. To rank as research, certain precautions need to be taken to ensure the validity of the findings, and the work of others in the same area needs to be consulted and compared. This might involve quite extensive reading, and the format for writing up research may also prove more time-consuming than expected.

Much handwriting research takes place in laboratory conditions, but if field research is considered more relevant, it is important to plan this very carefully to ensure that strict procedures are carried out. Test conditions must remain the same for each child in the sample, and the sample must be as widely representative of any group as possible. A research project may entail considerable organisation to ensure that enough children in each necessary category are included to make the findings significant.

There is, however, considerable value in carrying out simpler classroom-based school surveys of handwriting. By conducting such a survey anyone can observe, analyse and tabulate exactly what is happening in any particular classroom. All that is needed is to decide what should be observed and how this can be carried out. Some useful questions to ask might be:

1. Should each child be tested separately or can the required information be gathered in a whole class situation?

2. Is any kind of a questionnaire necessary or desirable?

3. Should a specific task be set, or will the conclusions be drawn from what can be observed in an everyday classroom situation?

These are very basic questions and there are no right or wrong answers. A quick look at a vital aspect of handwriting might provide more useful information than a lengthy survey of some other area. Although the survey might start with the intention of studying one aspect of handwriting, something might be discovered that could alter the direction of the survey. This could end up with an important find, something that deserves to be written up. Once again, there is a choice – a general article or a more academic paper. Whichever level is chosen, writing up findings helps to clarify the researcher's or observer's views. There are plenty of journals that might be willing to publish an article, and with luck publication may lead to an exchange of ideas with others who are interested in the same subject.

This part of the book provides ideas for surveys that would inform teachers and others of what is happening in many areas of children's handwriting. Such surveys could provide answers to key questions including how many pupils at any age are forming their letters incorrectly, or how valuable is a school model. Wherever possible, illustrations of teachers' surveys are given, to show how effective simple projects can be. In addition, there are several examples of different methods of presenting findings in simple graphs and tables.

Research methods

This second part of the book also presents a certain amount of statistical and visual evidence on a variety of the aspects of handwriting, to support the recommendations that are put forward. The evidence comes from my own extensive research project that looked simultaneously at letters, and the way children produced them. Little research had been done in this field so there was a lot of preliminary work to be done. Methods of observing, measuring and analysing such matters as penholds and paper position had to be evolved. When it came to letters, it was first necessary to decide what aspects of handwriting were measurable and what would only yield subjective judgements.

The devising of methods that could be carried out in almost any classroom could be considered just as valuable as the actual findings. Some of the planning that went into this project is detailed here. This is partly to show the method that led to my findings, and at the same time, to demonstrate how others could set about replicating this work in their own districts.

Research projects – a case study

The way a project is planned will inevitably affect the findings, so, in the case of my own project it was necessary from the start to evolve methods that would give a true picture of children's handwriting performance. Much handwriting research is carried out with computer-linked equipment in laboratories, but we cannot know how taking young children out of their usual surroundings and using unfamiliar writing implements alters their handwriting. It was decided therefore that all observation should take place in schools, in relaxed and natural surroundings.

Six primary schools were used in the investigation. They were chosen because each of them had a definite model or method that had been in use for several years. This meant that certain comparisons could be made between the resulting handwriting. Two secondary schools in the same district provided the older sample, so that some ex-pupils from the primary schools could be used to look at the possible long-term effects of some of the models. Approximately one hundred pupils were tested each time at three separate ages: 7+, 9+ and 15+. This gave a picture of what was happening:

1. After two years of handwriting instruction in infant school

2. After two years of instruction in joining letters in junior school

3. During the last year of compulsory education.

This may not seem a large sample, but each child was tested and photographed separately. Testing was only carried out in the morning in case tiredness should affect the results, and this field work alone took almost two years.

What was observed

Certain observations were made as each pupil performed a written task. Body posture and paper position were noted and penhold was carefully photographed. While the children were writing, the movement of each letter was observed and any unconventional movements were noted. This method would allow a tester to ask for any doubtful letter to be repeated in a word at the end of the formal test. Black ballpoint pens were used for the main task and they provided an additional safeguard. Had it been necessary to prove any suspect movement, this would have shown up through striations in the ink under a microscope. In the event this technique was not necessary.

The task

The primary and secondary pupils had slightly different tasks to perform, as well as different test sentences to write. There were three test sentences, typed on separate cards. They were presented in turn, and each child was told that the first two sentences were to be written at their normal writing speed. The younger children were allowed two practice attempts to eliminate as many spelling errors as possible, before being timed on the third attempt. The final sentence was to be written as fast as possible and no practice was necessary as it was a simple and well-known line from a nursery rhyme.

The secondary pupils were asked to write a sentence with their usual pen in case the use of a ballpoint should alter the movement of any letters. They also had three sentences to write, the first two at normal speed and the third as fast as possible. One practice was considered enough for these older pupils, before the first two sentences were timed. The third sentence was written once only.

It is hoped that these research methods will be repeated by other people in different regions so a more detailed picture of all our children's performance can be built up. None of it is complicated to carry out, enough information can be gathered quite easily and accurately in any school with no special equipment except a good hand-held camera to photograph the penholds. Some of the results have already been published in thesis or paper form and are listed below for anyone whose work requires that they have access to more statistical evidence or further references. This allows me to present the most relevant parts of the research in a more visual and practical way.

References

Sassoon R., Wing A. and Nimmo-Smith I., 'An Analysis of Children's Penholds', in Kao H.S.R., van Galen G.P. and Hoosain R. (eds.), *Graphonomics* (North Holland, 1986)

Sassoon R., 'Joins in Children's Handwriting, and the Effects of Different Models and Teaching Methods'. Thesis submitted for the Degree of Doctor of Philosophy, Department of Typography & Graphic Communication, University of Reading 1988

Sassoon R., Wing A. and Nimmo-Smith I., 'Developing Efficiency in Cursive Handwriting: An Analysis of 't' Crossing Behavior in Children', in Plamonden R., Suen C. and Simner M.(eds.), *Computer Recognition and Human Production of Handwriting* (World Scientific Publications, Singapore, 1989)

Sassoon R., 'The Effects of Teachers' Personal Handwriting on How They Produce School Models', in Wann J.P., Wing A.M. and Sovik N. (eds.), *Development of Graphic Skills* (Academic Press, 1990)

10 Looking at handwriting from different angles

Research that might affect educational planning should be as broad-based as possible. The educational, the physiological or psychological and the letterform perspectives of handwriting all have to be taken into consideration before a balanced understanding of children's needs can be reached.

Starting with the educational perspective, the performance of pupils is likely to reflect what they have been taught. It is not a good idea to pay too much attention to, or draw too many conclusions from research that does not take into account what training children have had. In such cases, the findings may only reflect habits that are the result of either bad or good teaching. If, for instance, a specialised survey showed up certain unusual details in left-handed behaviour, it would be essential to discover what strategies these pupils had been taught, before using such information as a basis for planning. The findings could reflect or be distorted by problems of those children who had not been helped to find suitable ways of dealing with left-handed posture in the first place. On the other hand, it is not a good idea to use the performance of pupils from one particularly good school as a measure of any aspect of handwriting, without taking into consideration how much time might have been spent on training the children, how informed the teachers were, or what particular models and methods had been used.

Taking the physiological and psychological aspects of handwriting into account

It is essential to understand that handwriting is the visible trace of a hand movement, so the working of the body must be taken into account when looking at handwriting. The term 'motor-perceptual skill' is sometimes used to describe the act of writing. This is self-explanatory, emphasising that both perception and production are involved. Handwriting is not just a matter of copying letters; the mind, the body and the emotions are all involved, and all these should be taken into consideration.

Separate aspects such as writing posture must be closely observed. These include not only how children sit but such details as penhold. Penhold and hand position inevitably affect the letters that are produced. Paper position also needs investigating because it may affect how the writer sits. Observing penhold can lead to an understanding of the effects of modern pens and looking at posture should lead, for instance, to an understanding of how classroom furniture might affect the way children sit. Each time a new feature is included, the subject gets more interesting.

If the psychological aspect is ignored, then those with complex problems may not have their interests taken into consideration. As the different tasks involved in putting letters on to paper are separated and the developmental aspects of writing are taken into consideration, it becomes clearer how so many problems can arise. The importance of systematic teaching becomes obvious, not only in ensuring that each stage is assimilated but in helping to pinpoint specific problems early enough to take remedial action. With this should come a more informed and sympathetic understanding of those who find the task difficult.

Understanding the letterform aspect of handwriting

The study of letterforms has been neglected for so many years that few people have enough understanding of letters to be able to observe, analyse, measure or compare them in an informed way. Where specialists in letterforms have intervened over children's handwriting it has often been to put forward their personal views of the ideal handwriting model. This has led to controversies that have contributed to even more handwriting problems, as the assumption always seemed to be that the model was all-important. An understanding of letters is essential in order to make the vital policy decisions about handwriting, or even everyday ones to help pupils to solve their problems. An understanding of the factors that affect legibility is also important. It is not just a matter of choosing a model and hoping that this will solve all the problems.

To understand letters it is important to observe them closely. It is a good idea to begin with separate basic letters, classifying them element by element. Details such as slant, proportion and height differentials that might previously have gone unobserved, soon become easier to pick out and analyse. Once each mark on the paper is translated into terms of movement and accepted as a separate action of the hand, such details as entry strokes or exit strokes assume more importance. It is then easier to judge the relative merits of different handwriting models.

Once accustomed to observing the movement of letters on paper, or even better, to watching children's hands as they move in forming those letters, the importance of teaching the correct movement of letters from the start becomes apparent. It does not take long to become expert at spotting the clues that indicate the point of entry and direction of stroke. Once this happens, the next step, explaining this to pupils and helping them to retrain, becomes much easier.

Joins get more and more complex as writing matures and becomes more personal, so once again it is best to start looking at straightforward ones first. By observing and analysing joins, the many different ways in which pupils adapt what they have been taught to suit their needs, become evident. In some aspects, our letters need to keep to the rules in order to be legible, but in others, the alphabet is flexible and can be manipulated to suit individual tastes and requirements. In the end, it becomes clear that the model itself is much less important than an understanding of how letters work. Then it is a matter of deciding what is essential to teach about letters, and what can be left to personal choice.

Separating the issues

In this part of the book, it is suggested that various key aspects of handwriting should be observed separately: first the movement of letters, joins and joining strokes and hand-writing models – how they are reproduced by teachers and then pupils; then speed, pencils and pens, penhold and posture and paper position.

It is then up to individuals how they use their observational skills or the information that they may have recorded.

11 Looking at the movement of letters

Why is it that our children have so much trouble with the basic movement of letters? It may be that many people just do not realise the importance of systematic teaching of movement in the early years. In order to be convinced of the seriousness of the situation they may need evidence of how prevalent movement faults are. The incorrect movement of letters is one of the simplest aspects of handwriting for any school to survey, but it could be one of the most important. It can show how many children at any age are displaying letters with an incorrect movement. This can inhibit the development of recognisable joins and is quite likely to result in illegible handwriting. The sooner movement faults are dealt with, the better.

A survey of incorrect movements can help in many ways. It may indicate cases of entire schools where insufficient grounding has been given in the movement of letters. Their pupils would need extra help before they were ready to join up their letters. As well as measuring the incorrect movements, a survey could give an indication of where the fault lay. Those involved in policy planning would have a useful measure, and possibly a tool for insisting on better teaching.

Definition of correct or incorrect movement

When setting up a survey, it is necessary to define exactly what is meant by the term 'correct' or 'incorrect movement'. Criteria may vary according to what you want to measure. If adherence to a specific model is being measured, then the decisions are easy, but otherwise there are likely to be plenty of stylistic differences that are (or anyhow should be) acceptable by teachers. The letters 'b','f', 'k' and 's' are perhaps those most likely to vary in their basic form from one school model to another. If children have been taught to use one form in a school and then have to move to another school, is it fair to make them change? In a survey you would have to decide whether to count a different form of a letter that may involve a different movement, as a fault.

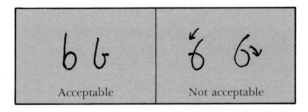

Different forms of the letter 'b'.

This already introduces two definitions of correct or incorrect: one that is essential to the development of an efficient, legible handwriting, and one involving stylistic issues where opinions might vary from person to person. Schools need to think carefully about this issue because it is just as hard for children to alter the movement of a perfectly acceptable but different form of a letter 'b' or 'f', as it is to change an unacceptable movement fault in a basic letter. Many children understandably resent having to change what they consider perfectly good letterforms – ones that might have been praised the previous term in their former school.

Whatever model is taught, children start at quite an early age to experiment, and often manage to find quite legible and acceptable forms that alter the movement of certain letters. These become more evident as children start to join their letters, but such differences are quite likely to pass unnoticed until someone starts to look into the details of handwriting performance. Surveying the details of letters should lead to an understanding of the differences between acceptable personal variations and those that will disrupt the flow of handwriting. In the end, what has been learned about handwriting may be just as important as the statistical findings from the survey.

The point of entry to letters

Some models indicate a recommended point of entry to letters, but not all. It may be left to the individual teacher to decide what is right or wrong – whether when demonstrating for teaching purposes or classifying for an analysis of letters. The point of entry to a letter can determine whether the movement is correct or incorrect. In some cases the decision is obvious, for example when deciding that an 'l' or an 'h' must start at the top of the ascender in the basic form rather than at the base. In other cases it is not so clear. The point of entry of the letter 'o' can vary considerably and cannot really be classified as correct or incorrect. The 'o' with its entry point at the top-right could be said to be based on the letter 'c' and is perhaps the most desirable. It might be said to lead to a letter that is less likely to become degraded when written at speed. An 'o' that starts at the centre-top is probably quite acceptable; only when its entry is top-left could it be termed as incorrect. Many adults start at this point and close their 'o's with a loop. A top-left entry would have to be criticised if it appeared in a teaching model, but in a survey such as is suggested here, these smaller variations of point of entry might not be worth recording unless they result in the bizarre kind of letters illustrated below.

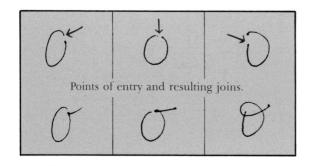

Points of entry and resulting joins.

An incorrect point of entry can affect related letters and joins.

For most purposes, an incorrect letter 'o' is one that either:

1. Starts at the baseline and moves either in a clockwise or anti-clockwise direction

2. Starts at the top and moves in a clockwise direction.

The advantages of individual testing

Individual testing is the best way of ensuring that the movement of letters is accurately recorded. It may be relatively easy to judge the point of entry and direction of stroke of separate letters if you watch a child while writing, but neither are easy to detect from a previously written sample.

When it comes to joined letters, it is more difficult to decide what is correct and what is not. It is not always possible to see what is happening, even by watching a teenager write. The advantage of individual testing is that you can always ask for a suspect letter to be repeated at the end of the formal task.

However closely you observe, you may become less sure of where to draw the line between what should be termed right or wrong. For instance, the entry to letters is affected by the height of the exit from the previous letter, so one common feature of teenage writing, the erosion of height differentials, can result in some unusual joins and entries. Idiosyncratic letterforms creep in as older children begin to experiment. When you take into account the effect that speed can have on the movement of joined letters, you cannot fail to notice personal alterations that add to the efficiency and maturity of handwriting. It may not be possible or desirable to say what is correct or incorrect, but it is important to be able to advise pupils when, for instance, they simplify movements so much, in the interest of efficiency, that their handwriting loses such features as are necessary for legibility. Nonetheless, any incorrect movement of the basic letters can usually be observed and quantified even at this stage. From the therapeutic point of view, it is never too late to help pupils alter incorrect basic movements, such as pushing letters up from the baseline.

Test sentences

The initial planning that goes into any project is going to affect the findings. Test sentences need to be designed carefully to suit the purpose of the survey. If the sole purpose is to count the number of movement faults in young children's separate letters, this is fairly easy. You will need words that are suited to the age group and to ensure that you include all the letters of the alphabet. It is often better not to try to fit them all into one sentence, but to have several short ones. Sentences such as 'the quick brown fox' may be adequate for older pupils, but the concentration of less commonly used letters and digraphs could make it an awkward and unrepresentative task for younger children.

Example of a small-scale teachers' survey

This small project on the formation of the letter 'f' was undertaken as voluntary homework by two teachers on a two-session, evening in-service course. It was not meant to take up much time and is included here to show how easy it is, and how much can be learned even from testing one key letter. The sample consisted of fifty top juniors aged ten years old from two schools. Twenty pupils came from School 'A' and thirty came from School 'B'. All the pupils were given appropriate sentences by their teachers to test the formation of the letter 'f'. Six pupils in all, four from School 'A' and two from School 'B' had problems with a basic letter 'f'. They either used a capital letter or demonstrated an incorrect movement.

If the letter 'f' is written with an incorrect movement, it cannot join successfully (1 and 2). Where the movement is correct they join easily at speed, either forwards or backwards (3 and 4).

Other problems arose when each pupil was asked to join their letter 'f' to the following letter. Sometimes incorrect height differentials produced an unsatisfactory join. This showed the two teachers how, even with a correct movement in basic letters, there are other factors to consider and that these get more important when letters are joined.

Research findings: what can be learned

Some of the findings from my research are shown here to illustrate ways of presenting the results of your survey.

Differences between schools

This graph shows the average number of movement faults in six schools, tabulated by age and school. This survey dealt with two different sets of children, but the totals of movement faults are a fair indication of the priorities that the infant schools feeding the six schools gave to the importance of teaching the correct movement of letters. In School 1 the improvement between the age of seven and nine suggests that a lot of valuable teaching time might have been wasted reteaching the correct movement of letters.

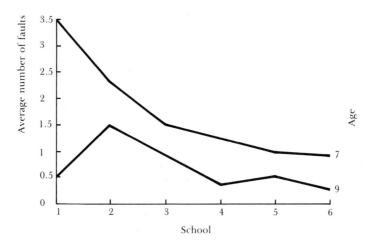

The average number of movement faults of seven- and nine-year-old pupils in each school.

The individual scores of the seven-year-olds might produce more useful information. This simple method tabulates how many children from each school displayed more than five letters with an incorrect movement.

School 1   2 pupils had 13 faults each   School 3   1 pupil had 6 faults
           1 pupil had 7 faults   School 4   no pupil had 5 faults
           1 pupil had 6 faults   School 5   no pupil had 5 faults
           1 pupil had 5 faults   School 6   no pupil had 5 faults
School 2   1 pupil had 8 faults
           1 pupil had 5 faults

This table shows clearly that some schools give less priority to the movement of letters than others. Any school that lets two children leave for junior school displaying thirteen faults and three more children with more than five faults, out of a total of fifteen pupils, must be giving a low priority to teaching the correct movement of letters.

The incidence of letters with an incorrect movement

It might be useful to know which letters were most often written with an incorrect movement. My findings from the younger pupils are shown below.

The letter 'd' 35   (plus 5 b/d reversals)   The letter 'o' 34   The letter 'u' 13

At secondary level, the 102 pupils averaged one fault each. The most frequent movement errors from the older pupils are set out below.

The letter 'u' 26   The letter 'o' 15   The letter 'a' 15

This survey looked at six primary schools and two secondary schools in one area. In no way is it suggested that the findings are a national or even a district average. Anyone wanting to find out what the position is in a specific school or area can easily conduct a survey using any or all of these methods.

12   Looking at joins

For any real understanding of handwriting it is essential to be fully aware of what joins are and how they work. When the writer lifts the pen between two letters and then repositions it, those letters appear as separated on the page. When the writer keeps the pen on the paper between letters, then they appear as joined letters. Sometimes that movement of the hand off the paper that resulted in separating the letters is almost the same as the movement that is recorded on the page by a join, but not always. The implications of these differences and the importance of the movement of the hand off the paper become apparent as the complexities of joins are explained.

Joins and joining strokes can be observed and counted with reasonable (but not infallible) accuracy so they can be a reliable measure to use in a survey. First it is necessary to define the different stages of letters that might be involved in a survey of joins and joining strokes.

1. Joined letters – these occur when there is no pen lift involved, whatever the form of the letter or the variation of the join.

2. Separate letters – there would need to be three classifications:
    a) A letter with a straight terminal
    b) A letter with an integral exit or joining stroke
    c) A letter that touches the following letter but cannot count as a join because a penlift is involved.

Looking into the details of joins and joining strokes, separating and counting them, is a good way of getting an understanding of the mechanics of what is often loosely termed 'cursive' or 'joined-up writing'.

What a survey might disclose

A simple count of joins will show how many children at any age are joining letters. This can then be interpreted in several ways. It could be a certain amount of use when looking at the performance in one school age by age. The average number of joins could be compared or individual scores could be investigated. This might well illustrate how pupils who have received the same training demonstrate considerable variability in their use of joins. If the writers had been timed, it would be possible to see if those who wrote the fastest were those with the most joins. Those findings might be quite a surprise, as the fastest writing often has less joins than expected. Although it is very difficult to assess the effects of joins on the quality of handwriting, the differences between those who have joined almost all their letters and those who have taken more penlifts can be interesting. The incidence of certain joins, perhaps comparing the performance of boys and girls, can lead to an understanding of how writers find and use the joins that work best with their personal letterforms. The differences between the joins of left-handers and right-handers might show how left-handers modify some joins to suit the right-to-left directional strokes that come more easily to them.

When the overall pattern of joins between several schools can be compared, the influence of different models and teaching methods might be reflected in a survey.

The movement between letters

When the details of the terminals of separate letters are classified it is easier to judge the possible effects of different models on the development of an efficient movement between letters. This efficiency of movement is what is needed in handwriting. Providing the hand moves in the right way beween letters, it is not so important whether a visible join occurs or not.

Joining strokes (or exit strokes) are an earlier stage in the development of joins. Counting them can show up the differences in the handwriting of children who have been taught letters with exit strokes from the beginning, and those who have tried to add exit strokes to print script letters later on. Two separate issues are involved in the development of joining strokes, one physiological and one concerning the written trace. The physiological issue concerns the hand, and the training and automating of a motor movement. The first model that children are taught not only affects the way their letters look but is likely to affect the way they use their hands. Where print script is taught, young children are encouraged to end the down strokes neatly, and with maximum pressure, on the base line. If this abrupt movement is automated, it is often difficult for the writer to change to the onward flowing movement that is required for any level of joined handwriting. The proportion of pupils who find this changeover hard to achieve can be assessed by the simple method of counting the exit strokes on the letters of junior school children who are being taught to join their letters.

How it begins –

adding exit strokes to print script at seven.

The result – inefficient joins at fifteen.

The pen pressure must also be taken into consideration, because the point where maximum pressure is exerted might affect how children develop their joins. The pressure pattern becomes automated in the same way as other features of handwriting. This pressure may be invisible to all but the most experienced eyes, but its reliability as an aspect of personal handwriting is used by forensic experts in their battle against forgers. If the writer becomes used to concentrating maximum pen pressure on the base line, this may be the factor that becomes hardest to alter. The difficulty would occur in simultaneously changing direction to form a join and releasing pressure. This difficulty can easily be spotted in the awkward and inefficient joins that result.

45

Where exit strokes have been taught from the start, there is little pressure at the baseline and not much on the upstroke. This should contribute towards the development of spontaneous baseline joins as children speed up their writing. In addition, these joining strokes may well both space letters better and lead to joining in the most relaxed way. This cannot be measured but the theory can be illustrated.

What started as a simple count of joins has turned into an examination of some of the most subtle but important differences in determining whether a handwriting works smoothly or not. Finally, it is evident that a letter, that ends in such a way that the trajectory of the pen is in the wrong direction to progress logically to the start of the following letter, is likely to produce an inefficient movement in the air. It may not be possible to measure this wasted movement and momentum without special equipment, but it is not too difficult for an informed observer to work out what is likely to go wrong, and, if necessary, explain this to the writer.

The effects of speed on joins

The comparison between joins in fast writing and writing at normal speed can provide an insight into how fast writing can increase in efficiency. Within, for instance, the word 'the', writers often make alterations at speed that completely change the movement between the letters 't–h'. This saves time but does not necessarily affect the legibility. It is possible to understand a little about the way our motor memory works, because these changes of movement seem to be quite unconscious, they are often retrieved from memory only when extra speed is called for. These findings raise as many questions as they answer. If there are different and personal ways of joining letters then should all pupils be introduced to them and encouraged to choose those that work well with their own letterforms? Knowledge of a variety of personal joins can help when it is necessary to guide pupils towards legible shortcuts in their writing. This is a common problem when extra speed becomes a priority in secondary school.

Findings from research into joins

A few of my research findings are shown here to lend support to many of the ideas expressed in this book, and also to show teachers and others ways of presenting the results from their own surveys.

There is one way of measuring joins that is so simple, that the necessary information can be gathered in a few moments and quickly worked out to show the children's score on a ruled chart. Pupils can be given a standard sentence and then each of the possible joins counted. When the sentence is designed, a variety of different digraphs should be included, but it is a good idea to repeat one or two of them. This makes it possible to see how consistent individual children are in the use of the same join.

There were three instances in my test sentence for junior schools where the same pair of letters occurred in different positions in a word or in different words. In the sentence 'Tom is kicking the ball back to Kate', the letters 'k–i' appeared twice in the word 'kicking', 'c–k' appeared in 'kicking' and in 'back', and 'b-a' appeared in 'ball' and 'back'. The chart shows that those pairs of letters sometimes had different scores within the six schools taking part in this investigation. The pair 'k-i' showed most variation as would be expected, confirming similar studies of adult writing where two letters in different positions in words tend to vary in their degree of joining.

The individual school charts are not illustrated here, but the combined one is detailed enough to show how the incidence of joins varies not only between schools and between pupils, but within the performance of most pupils, whatever the model taught.

School	1	2	3	4	5	6	Average %
o–m	57	13	33	69	80	86	56.3
i–s	59	13	40	25	64	95	49.3
k–i	39	0	50	38	40	72	39.8
k–i	44	13	50	44	53	82	47.7
i–c	57	0	47	44	73	95	52.7
c–k	22	0	40	44	73	86	44.2
c–k	24	13	33	44	80	86	46.7
i–n	66	25	47	56	86	95	62.5
n–g	35	13	40	31	86	91	49.3
t–h	30	25	53	44	80	100	55.3
h–e	83	50	53	88	93	100	77.8
b–a	0	0	0	19	27	95	23.5
b–a	0	0	0	19	20	95	22.3
a–l	54	50	60	88	93	100	72.5
l–l	52	13	53	63	80	95	59.3
a–c	55	0	33	50	86	86	51.7
t–o	30	13	40	38	80	68	43.8
a–t	66	25	53	63	86	95	64.9
t–e	44	13	40	56	73	100	52.3
Average %	44	14	40	47	71	91	

This table shows the incidence of joins school by school. The results are shown as a percentage of pupils, classified by school and type of join, rounded to the nearest decimal point. The average of joins per school and the average incidence of each join are also shown as percentages.

Details of joining performance in junior schools

In a more complicated study, three joins were studied in detail. The joins that were chosen were l-l, a-c and o-o, representing one of each of three kinds of joins: baseline, reverse and top. The joins were quantified, wherever possible, both at normal speed and when children were writing as fast as possible. The baseline and reverse joins were each written twice at normal speed, and once as fast as possible. The top join was written twice at normal speed making a total of eleven measured joins.

Average number of joins

Age	Pupils	Joins	Average	Out of
7	92	206	2.24	11
9	101	392	3.88	11

This is a very simple analysis for anyone to do. If it were carried out throughout a school, it would give a good idea of how well and when pupils were starting to join their letters.

The influence of different models and methods on the amount of joining becomes clear when the results are shown school by school as seen in the tables below. Schools 1 and 2 taught italic with an emphasis right through the junior school on keeping to the model. School 3 taught from the Ruth Fagg, *Everyday Handwriting Copybooks* (Hodder and Stoughton, 1965) and School 4 was beginning to adopt a similar method, but based on suggestions from the Rosemary Sassoon, *Practical Guide to Children's Handwriting* (Thames and Hudson, 1982). These two schools put less emphasis on copying a model and more on first exit strokes and then joins from the age of seven. Schools 5 and 6 used the Marion Richardson, *Writing and Writing Patterns* (Hodder and Stoughton, 1935). School 5 had adapted the model to their own needs and started with separate letters with exit strokes. School 6 kept strictly to the model, so from the time children started school at five, they were encouraged to join their letters. The schools are roughly rated from 1–6 in order of how much emphasis they put on exit strokes and joins, bearing in mind that in Schools 1–4 the pupils had been taught print script in infant school while in School 5 they had started with letters with exit stroke and in School 6 joins were taught from the start.

Average of joins school by school

School	Pupils	Joins	Average of joins
7-year-old pupils			
1	15	1	0.07
2	10	1	0.10
3	18	0	0
4	16	0	0
5	16	33	2.06
6	17	171	10.06

School	Pupils	Joins	Average of joins
9-year-old pupils			
1	23	106	4.60
2	10	31	3.10
3	15	71	4.73
4	16	106	6.63
5	15	136	9.07
6	22	210	9.55

School 6 might not be typical of schools in Great Britain because few schools start to teach joined letters from the age of five years old. Even so it is evident that the earlier joining strokes were stressed without too much emphasis on a model, the more joins there were later on. Emphasis on an italic model did not seem to encourage the development of joins, despite the fact that both italic models had exit strokes on their letters.

The incidence of joins   The incidence of the three joins can easily be tabulated by age and school and could provide useful information. The results from the junior schools did not reveal enough of interest to reproduce them here in full, but overall the incidence of the three joins were as follows:

Age	l-l	a-c	o-o
7	56	57	57
9	213	165	173

These figures become more interesting once they are compared with incidence of joins in secondary schools.

The development of the 'l-l' join.   It might be useful to investigate the different stages of the development of each join. The 'l-l' join is used as an example of this method. The terminal of the first of the two 'l's in the pair is counted, the terminal of the second 'l' is not counted as it does not affect the join. This analysis tabulates how many children of each age in each school write the first letter in that pair as:

1. A straight letter with no exit stroke at the base

2. A letter with an exit stroke at the base

3. A letter with an exit stroke that touches the following letter

4. A letter that joins to the following letter.

Two instances are scored for each pupil: once where the two letters are written at normal speed and once where they are written as fast as possible.

'l-l' join at normal speed – 7-year-old pupils

	1. Straight	2. Exit	3. Touch	4. Join	
School 1	14	1	0	0	
School 2	3	7	0	0	
School 3	8	9	0	0	(-1)
School 4	7	9	0	0	
School 5	7	7	0	2	
School 6	1	0	0	16	
Totals	40	33	0	18	

'l-l' join as fast as possible – 7-year-old pupils

	1. Straight	2. Exit	3. Touch	4. Join
School 1	9	4	1	1
School 2	4	6	0	0
School 3	10	8	0	0
School 4	7	9	0	0
School 5	7	3	1	5
School 6	1	0	0	16
Totals	38	30	2	22

	1. Straight	2. Exit	3. Touch	4. Join
School 1	3	6	3	11
School 2	2	3	2	3
School 3	3	4	0	8
School 4	2	1	0	13
School 5	2	0	0	13
School 6	0	0	0	22
Totals	12	14	5	70

'l–l' join as fast as possible – 9-year-old pupils

	1. Straight	2. Exit	3. Touch	4. Join
School 1	6	8	1	8
School 2	3	4	0	3
School 3	3	5	0	7
School 4	2	1	0	13
School 5	2	1	0	12
School 6	0	0	0	22
Totals	16	19	1	65

These tables allow some other useful details to be observed about the performance of the six schools. The detailed way of looking at terminals showed, for instance, that contrary to expectation, letters do not always join more at speed. In School 1, the letters of nine-year-olds joined and touched less at speed. This might suggest that the flowing onward movement did not come as naturally to them at speed as it does to those who have been taught with an exit stroke from the start, or have had this point sufficiently stressed at seven years old. It might also signal that the increased emphasis on the italic model inhibited joins at speed, but the sample is too small to draw any conclusions.

Exaggerating an italic model by emphasising the triangular shape can affect joins.

Secondary school joins

The survey of joins in secondary school pupils' handwriting looked at equal numbers of boys and girls coming from a variety of primary schools. Some pupils had moved into the area from other parts of Great Britain and even a few from other countries. The same three joins were investigated in detail, both at normal speed and as fast as possible: 'l–l', 'a–c' and 'o–o'. The first table shows the total number of joins recorded (twice each at normal speed and once each as fast as possible).

Pupils	Joins	Average	Out of
104	425	4.09	9

When the total is divided between the boys and girls the first interesting point is shown.

	Total	Average of joins
Boys (52)	224	4.3
Girls (52)	201	3.9

There is little difference between the boys and girls. However, if you ask teachers they will usually assure you that girls' writing joins much less than boys'. A quick look at my examples might suggest the same thing. When the incidence of joins is counted, the reason for this apparent contradiction between the cursory 'look' of the examples and the closeness of the totals of joins becomes clearer.

	'l–l'	'a–c'	'o–o'
Boys	88	70	66
Girls	116	25	20

Now it is evident that the girls had a much higher proportion of baseline joins than the boys, but a lower proportion of reverse and top joins. Perhaps it is unwise to read too much into this sample but what this suggests to me is really only common sense. Teenage girls have on the whole 'fatter' letters than boys. They also have a somewhat different attitude to what they term 'neatness'. Girls join along the baseline most frequently because this is the easiest join. The reverse join is especially inefficient with fat letters and might look untidy. (It was noticeable that the few girls with narrow slanting letters had a more even distribution of the three joins within their total.) The examples showed that the girls took penlifts more often before letters requiring reverse joins. This would make their writing appear less joined because adults get most of their information from scanning the top of a line of letters. Less attention is paid to the information along the baseline.

David will pass this set of keys back afterwards.

Boys often joined everything regardless of the effect.

David will pass this set of keys back afterwards

Girls were neater, with more baseline joins.

51

The difference between the joins at speed and the joins at normal speed did not provide interesting statistics. All they showed was that twenty-five additional pairs of letters were joined at speed, but on the other hand twelve pairs that had been joined at normal speed were left unjoined at speed. The importance can only be shown in the illustrations. Speed produced increased efficiency in various ways. Sometimes the effects of speed altered the handwriting so much that it was hard to believe that both samples had been written by the same writer. In other cases, details of the personal joins that were developed at speed needed to be scrutinised to understand the importance of the findings.

The monkeys and in the zoo need just extra food. Jack is running down the hill to quickly.

Slow writing and fast writing by the same person may look quite different.

back back   will will   food. food.
Jack   is running   down the hill too quickly

On the other hand, fast writing can look the same but be much more joined.

Conclusion

My own research did not set out to show that joins have any special virtue, or that more joins are necessarily more desirable overall than less joins in certain handwriting. My own view has always been that joins usually facilitate the development of efficient legible handwriting, so children should learn them all, but then be encouraged to join when comfortable. The findings could be considered as support for these views, in that they present considerable personal variability in all the analyses carried out.

Simple methods of analysing joins have now been detailed. This makes it easier to learn from pupils' writing about the variability of joins and other details of how letters behave in different circumstances. It will soon become evident when this variability, that most people would accept as inevitable and probably desirable in adult handwriting, is beneficial and when it perhaps goes too far. Once this is understood, the way is open for teachers to guide their pupils in an informed way, not imposing joins for the sake of joining but showing where they should aid speed and efficiency. At the same time, educational planners, having surveyed an area and perhaps found too little joining, might consider that the solution should be to revert to teaching a form of continuous cursive. This would be jumping from one extreme to another, and might have just as undesirable consequences, as having too few joins.

13 Looking at handwriting models

Handwriting models are used in different ways. In some schools teachers and pupils are supposed to copy them closely, whereas in other schools they are used only as a rough guide. It sometimes happens that a school may think that pupils are following the model closely and profiting from the ideas behind the specific alphabet. On closer inspection it may become evident that both teachers and pupils are perceiving and/or producing something quite different. It may be a good idea to investigate what pupils are learning from the use of a particular model, and whether it is to their advantage or not. A method of analysing the letters of models, and the letters of those who have used them, will be required. Separating the different elements of letters is a good starting point.

This way of analysing, element by element, is a good way of learning more about letters. A school-based survey might not need as many elements as are shown here. Just two, the slant of letters such as 'l' and the proportion of the letter 'o' might be enough to show how well a model is being understood by teachers, then taught or being taken up by the pupils. Looking into the details of letters in this way, brings into focus features such as entry and exit strokes. Once they are noticed, they also begin to assume importance when investigating how teachers or pupils reproduce other elements of a model. The next stage, which can produce some nasty shocks, is to notice how personal deviations from the model on the part of teachers, affect their pupils' handwriting.

The influence of teachers' personal handwriting

Teachers often say how difficult it is to alter their own blackboard demonstrations and handwriting to comply with a different model when they change schools. This is quite understandable; forensic research illustrates the elements that adults find difficult to alter in handwriting. It is the difficulty in altering these elements that makes it possible to detect forgeries. It is important to understand not only the influence of teachers' personal handwriting on their representations of the school model, but how this, in turn, might influence their pupils' handwriting. I carried out some research into this with teachers at in-service sessions all over the country. The teachers were asked to 'take down' three sentences. They were then asked to write the same sentences again in the model that they taught their pupils. Personal handwriting and the teachers' representations of the model could then be compared. All examples that showed a joined-up model were discarded, leaving over a hundred examples of teachers' representations of print script. Initially, three elements of each pair of examples were looked at:

1. Slant

2. Proportion of the letter 'o'

3. The relationship between the 'x' height and ascender height, i.e. the difference between the letters 'i' and 'l', etc.

In the end, the slant alone was sufficient to demonstrate how much personal handwriting can affect reproduction of a model. All the teachers whose personal handwriting sloped backwards, had a backward slant in their representations of print script.

Several other details were looked at, such as the point of entry of personal handwriting and its affect on how teachers reproduce a model.

Some aspects of letters seemed easy for the teachers to alter. All but one of them, who used an undercurve 'b' in their personal handwriting, managed to change to a closed 'b' in the classroom.

the ball back	the ball back
the ball back	the ball back
the ball back	the ball back

Teachers altered their personal form of the letters 'b' and 'k' to write print script.

A detailed investigation of teachers in six local schools confirmed the findings of the national sample. The fourteen teachers whose examples could be used, showed that when copying the school model, none of them altered the slant of their personal handwriting. Seven of them had a personal handwriting that sloped forward, corresponding with the models. Seven did not slope forward, five of these wrote with upright letters and two slanted backwards. All of them produced a print script that sloped in the same way as their personal handwriting.

and Jill went up the hill
and Jill went up the hill

and Jill went up the hill
and Jill went up the hill

and Jill went up the hill.
and Jill went up the hill

When teachers' personal handwriting sloped backwards, so did their representations of the school model.

Elements	Model	Teacher 1	Teacher 2	Teacher 3
Slant	h k	hill	hill	hill
Proportion	o	oo	oo	oo
Ascenders	j g d	ball	ball	ball
Descenders		ing	ing	ing
Crossbar	tw	th	th	th
Entry	m r	is	is	is
Exit	a w	hiw	hiw	hiw
Arches	n u	n u	n u	n u
'e'	e	he	he	he
'b' and 'p'	b p	b p	b p	b p

A modified Marion Richardson model and three teachers' representations of it, analysed element by element.

How this could affect pupils

If the teachers are not perceiving or producing certain important elements of a model, it is unlikely that the pupils will profit from its use. Here is just one example, a case where the pupils were using the well-known Marion Richardson handwriting books. As the analysis on page 55 showed, the model has a slight forward slant, and the letter 'o' is not round but oval. A close look at the handwriting of twenty-two nine-year-old pupils showed that no pupil had a consistent forward slant, and that more than half of them sloped backwards. A scrutiny of the letter 'o' also showed that few of the pupils reproduced the proportions of the letters in the model.

A survey of teachers' reproductions of the school model could be carried out in any staffroom, but it would be better to use the findings to further the understanding of the complexities of handwriting, rather than to imply criticism of any member of staff. A constructive outcome from looking at the effect teachers' personal deviations from the model might have on pupils' handwriting work could be an understanding of how pupils are likely to pick up some of their teachers' stylistic habits. It is important to be aware of this and to try not to use any idiosyncratic letters or movements when demonstrating on the blackboard or writing in children's books.

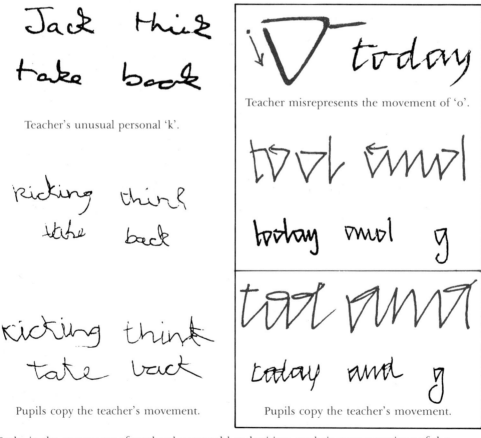

Teacher's unusual personal 'k'.

Teacher misrepresents the movement of 'o'.

Pupils copy the teacher's movement.

Pupils copy the teacher's movement.

Faults in the movement of teachers' personal handwriting, or their representations of the school model, can be picked up and copied by their pupils.

The effects of models on pupils' handwriting

It is important to find out what effects any specific model or method might have on pupils' handwriting later on in life. It is then possible to judge whether or not the handwriting training that children are having in primary school is likely to be of benefit later on. Liaison between primary and secondary schools can result in considerable advantages for all concerned. Many secondary schools include pupils who have been taught a variety of models, so secondary school teachers would be in a good position to advise on the possible long-term consequences of teaching certain models. It might be possible for primary schools to trace some of their ex-pupils and survey their views, and perhaps analyse their handwriting towards the end of their school days. It is not too difficult to carry out such a survey. The findings could give a valuable insight into the needs of our older pupils, and enable primary schools to modify their handwriting policies to prepare their pupils for the task ahead.

The forward slant and oval 'o' of Marion Richardson's model misrepresented by children.

Italic writing with least elements at 15+.

Italic writing with most elements at 15+.

Findings from research into school leavers' handwriting

My investigation dealt with six primary schools and two secondary schools in the same district. Some pupils who appeared in the sample from the secondary schools had previously attended one of the six primary schools. Fourteen pupils in the last year of compulsory education, were found to have attended one or other of the two primary schools where italic handwriting was taught. In order to trace how much the taught model had affected the pupils' handwriting, it was first necessary to decide which elements of the model should be looked at. Five of the elements from the analysis appear on page 58:

1. Forward slant

2. Letter proportion based on an oval

3. An acute exit stroke

4. Arches that spring from the stem of a downstroke

5. A two-stroke 'e'.

They were used to trace the influence of an italic model on school leavers' handwriting.

Teenagers' writing is not always consistent, so a three-point scale was used for this analysis:

Where the element predominates in the handwriting: Score 1
Where the element occurs sometimes: Score 0.5
Where the element is absent: Score 0.

Pupil	Elements of italic					Total
	1	2	3	4	5	
1	0	0	0	0	0	0
2	0	0	0	0	0	0
3	0	0	0	0	1	1
4	0	0.5	0.5	0	0	1
5	0	1	0	0	0	1
6	0	0.5	0	0.5	0	1
7	0.5	0.5	0	0.5	0	1.5
8	0	1	0	1	0	2
9	1	0.5	0.5	0.5	0	2.5
10	0	0.5	1	1	0	2.5
11	1	1	0	0.5	0	2.5
12	1	0.5	0	1	0	2.5
13	1	1	0.5	0.5	0	3
14	0	1	1	1	0	3
Totals out of a possible 70	4.5	8	3.5	6.5	1	23.5

This table shows that the most lasting effect of teaching italic within this sample was forward-sloping letters. The illustrations on page 57 show how little some writing resembled italic.

The pupils were asked for their views on italic as a teaching model, and most of them made comments. The replies revealed perhaps more than the table.

Pupil 2 said she did italic at school but did not take it home.
Pupils 4 and 5 said they did it a primary school but 'left it behind' before secondary school.
Pupil 6 said he did not like italic, and that it was too slow.
Pupil 8 had learning difficulties so perhaps he was not a typical example.
Pupil 9 did not consider his writing to be italic and said that he thought italic was upright.
Pupil 11 said that he found italic difficult, and felt that he was held back by its rigidity.
Pupil 12 could only remember that he got ink all over his fingers from the compulsory, broad-edge nibbed fountain pens, and now he used a ballpoint.

The only positive response came from Pupil 13, who said that she had dropped italic for the first three years in secondary school but had now 'gone back to it'. Her writing was the most flowing of all the examples. It suggests that when italic is adopted voluntarily and selectively by those who are attracted to it, the result can be efficient and personal.

These findings are from a very small sample. However, pupils' comments should not be ignored. Whatever model is being used, if it does not suit a considerable proportion of the children, then maybe it is doing more harm than good.

14 Looking at speed

Speed is one of the easiest aspects of handwriting to test, but one where the findings require careful interpretation. A group of pupils, a whole school even, can be tested by giving them a passage to write out, stopping after a certain time and calculating how many letters each pupil has written per minute. It is then simple to say how many letters are written on average at each age, but it is important to be clear about what this proves; only that a certain set of pupils has written so many words per minute, while performing a certain task on a certain day, in certain conditions. The task might have been quite different from the task that those children usually perform in class; the 'norm' may not be at all suitable for assessing what children should be able to do in everyday life. Sometimes in speed tests, pupils are instructed to repeat a three, four or five word phrase for several minutes. The total number of letters produced in this way are then averaged out to show how many the children are capable of producing per minute. This cannot reflect a true picture of what should be expected of children, as it is in no way representative of a usual writing task. This method cannot even be a good test of motor performance, because the repetition of so few letters is involved. The other problem about relying on such tests is that there is likely to be a trade off between speed and legibility, and that there is no reliable test of quality to balance this. When children are tested individually, these matters are much easier to understand.

Speed tests in secondary schools

Problems remain even at secondary level; if pupils are given a repetitive task to minimise spelling or other problems, then the findings from such tests may not be relevant to the more usual handwriting tasks in school. If 'creative' writing is timed, then it may not be the act of writing itself that is accurately reflected. When quoting from research findings, it is important to find out how any particular speed norms were reached. While suggesting that any generalised speed norm might be deceptive, speed differentials can be an indicator and useful in diagnosis. Supposing, in the simplest of group speed tests, several pupils appeared much slower than their peers, an individual retest might reveal the reason. This could reveal anything from a visual problem, a motor problem, to a penhold that prevented fast writing. On the other hand, it might reveal that certain pupils gave a high priority for neatness or beauty in handwriting and preferred to provide a smaller, but 'better' sample. If the task had included a creative element, to simulate more closely the usual usage of handwriting, then further investigation might reveal that the 'slow' writer might be a deep thinker who produced fewer letters but more profound thoughts. On the other hand it might indicate that the speed (indicated by an average of letters per minute) was inhibited by spelling or difficulties in expressing thoughts in writing, or even a deeply rooted dislike of putting pen to paper which is often the result of constant criticism.

This should not discourage anyone from using speed tests where appropriate. If the test is designed in such a way to fit the purpose of the survey, then the findings can be valuable in assessing individual needs. As for norms, maybe handwriting is such a personal matter that speed norms are neither accurate indicators, nor particularly desirable.

Designing a speed test

General points to watch when designing a test sentence, and setting up a speed test:

1. That any words used should be within the spelling capacity of the age group concerned.

2. That a representative selection of commonly used letters and digraphs should be used. (Sentences that are designed to include every letter of the alphabet sometimes have uncommon combinations that might disrupt the results with young children.)

3. That a certain amount of rehearsal should be built into the task, but not so much that the writer either becomes bored, or writes in such an automatic way that it becomes an unrealistic task.

4. How the task is presented might affect the findings. If it is written on the blackboard then those with visual problems and those who find difficulty relating from one plane to another might be at a disadvantage. A clearly typed (or written) copy for each pupil would be better, and in some 'whole class' situations, it might be a good idea to read the passage out loud as well as to provide individual copies.

Research findings

In my own research project, all children were tested individually, so it was possible to observe their reactions to the task and see how these might affect the accuracy of the speeds. During the testing, the younger children revealed that spelling, poor concentration and lack of copying strategies often influenced how fast they were able to write. It was not always an accurate measure of the act of writing, even when a rehearsal had been built into the task. Some children could be observed to race against the clock even when instructed to write at normal speed. This was particularly noticeable in a set of boys in a rather competitive school. All these factors led me to think that the results of speed tests of young childrens' handwriting should be treated with caution.

Speed tests of older pupils permitted some useful findings to be reported, but again these findings should be considered specific both to the task and the sample when averages are quoted. Where older pupils responded more accurately to the instructions that were given to them, interesting comparisons were possible, in particular those that showed the influence of speed on joins and other elements of handwriting. The speeds from my own research were published in Sassoon, Wing and Nimmo-Smith, 'An Analysis of Children's Penholds' (1986, see page 36) where they were used to measure the effects of different penholds. They succeeded in showing (within the sample of 400) that unconventional penholds permitted writers to produce as high an average of letters per minute as conventional tripod penholds. It was also shown that all three age groups were able to speed up by about twenty-five per cent when asked to write as fast as possible. Neither of these analyses were designed to take the quality of the resulting letters into account.

15 Looking at pencils and pens

In the first part of this book it was suggested that children should be given a choice of writing implements. In some schools this already happens but in others this is not the case. Sometimes it is teachers who make the decision, but elsewhere it may be up to the district or county supplies officer to decide what should be available for children of different ages. The decision about what to stock could be more effectively based on local surveys of children's preferences, but unfortunately many infant schools in Great Britain are only supplied with fat pencils, because some research in the past suggested that these were best for young children. No-one can quote a specific reference for this research; moreover the majority of infant teachers find that fat pencils are not beneficial to all children, and a distinct disadvantage to many. It is possible that the supplier who can provide pens at a reasonable price may get the contract to supply schools in any particular area, and it may not be in the interest of that supplier to produce more than one size of handle. Although standard pencils are available for older pupils, the only pens available in many parts of Great Britain have fat handles.

Letting children choose

If children are asked for their preferences, they often choose standard or even quite thin pens but, because of financial constraints, many children are writing with pens that do not feel comfortable, or work well for their writing. It is quite simple to ask pupils what they prefer, and young children are surprisingly specific about their likes and dislikes both of pen size and pen point. If more people undertook such surveys, they might help to change entrenched ideas about the suitability of pens and pencils for school children.

A selection of pencils is needed to test infants: large fat pencils, standard-sized ones (both round and hexagonal if possible) and also triangular ones. These triangular pencils are easily available and increasingly used in infant classes, so it would be a good idea to find out what the children think of them. To widen the survey, soft and hard leads, and perhaps a few fibre-tipped pens could be included for the top infants.

Teachers' surveys

This kind of survey will not only produce useful statistics, but by asking young children about their preferences, you may learn more about the children themselves.

An infant teacher asked six five-year-olds in their first month at school what they liked to write with. They drew a picture and then wrote their names and the teacher transcribed their replies:

> Pupil 1 liked crayons best because he had them at home.
> Pupil 2 liked crayons because they are brightly coloured; thick for colouring but thin for her work book (presumably her writing book).
> Pupil 3 liked coloured pencils best, and hated crayons because they are too thick.
> Pupil 4 liked crayons best. He had felt-tipped pens at home but no pencils.

Ashley uses coloured pencils and hates wax crayons because they are too thick. The line quality of his letters is already apparent, and his early appreciation of particular tools may indicate an artistic talent.

ASHLEY

David likes wax crayons best because he has them at home. Are the fat crayons partly to blame for his crude letters? A choice of pencils from an early age and teaching children that letters need more precise movements than colouring and free drawing, might be indicated here.

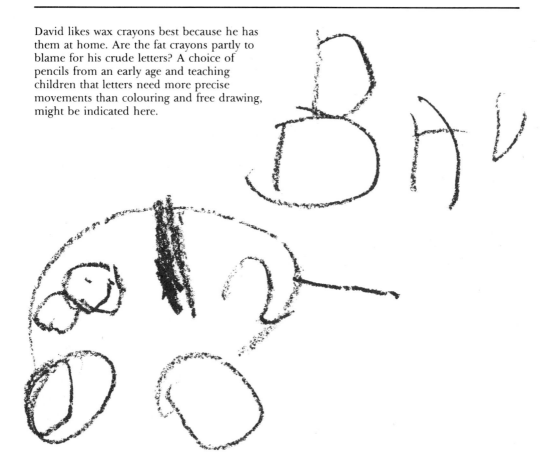

Pupil 5 liked thick crayons but also said somewhat confusingly that she 'did not like pencils because it gets on her hands'.

Pupil 6 liked crayons and pencils of any size but for no particular reason.

Children in the first months of schooling cannot be expected to give rational reasons for their preferences, but several interesting points arose even from this small sample.

The examples of drawings with attempts at name-writing suggested that some of the children did not differentiate between tools for colouring in and those for writing. It would be useful for teachers to observe whether such children used the necessary different strategies for the precision task of writing letters, and the less precise task of colouring. Few people would deny that fat crayons are good for pre-school children to use for colouring, maybe that is the origin of the belief that they are also the best tool for writing.

It is quite easy to give slightly older children a trial pack of pens and pencils to try out, with a simple chart to record their preferences. It is also informative to observe their attitudes to such a task. One teacher of seven-year-old pupils observed:

1. The children were surprised at being asked to choose.

2. Given a mixed pack of pens and pencils some children asked 'Does it have to be pencils?'

3. Some, used only to pencils, found the pens difficult at first.

4. Others once they realised that they were free to choose, discarded the pencils and concentrated on the pens.

5. The pack included blue points; the question arose 'Does writing always have to be black, can we have colours too?'

All these points could lead on to a class discussion on implements and writing.

The next stage can be to ask pupils why they prefer their first choice from a variety of pens and pencils. Two groups of junior school pupils aged seven to eight, and nine to ten, were given a pack of ten implements to choose from. The younger group all made a definite choice but their reasons were somewhat simplistic.

The older group were usually able to describe quite clearly why they made their choice. An overhead projector pen was mistakenly included in their trial pack, making eleven choices in all. Somewhat comically, the overhead protector pen became the first choice of two pupils.

The pen-preference test

My own research was aimed at persuading county suppliers to consider the benefits of including different-sized pencils for infants in their catalogue, as well as variety of pen sizes for junior schools. An informal survey had already shown that all through primary school most children preferred standard-sized pencils and pens with similar-sized barrels, not extra thick ones. Teachers noticed that children whose parents could afford them brought slimline felt-tipped pens and pencils into infant classes, and also remarked that they considered that fat pencils were difficult to manage. Many of the junior pupils

The best pen was the over head protecter cause it was very easy too write with

I LIK this pen Be cause it Dunt leck

I Like this pen becouse
it di nice and bine and i can right
niba with th tiner pens

because I had more control over the pen. And I also liked because the end is skinny and easy to hold.

I prefor writting in cartrige pen becouse It is confteble and I can wright faster with it

I chose this pen because it feels comfterble and I Like the way it's thick when it comes out.

I like this pen bacause I can write frster.

These nine-year-olds were given ten pens (plus the overhead projector pen) to try. They indicated their different preferences and the precise reasons behind their choice.

complained that they did not find the fat pens comfortable to use. To make any real impact on entrenched opinions accurate research must be undertaken, so a simple but carefully constructed pen-preference test was included in my research project.

Three fibre-tipped pens with similar points, but different-sized barrels were used. The approximate circumferences were:

Pen 1 (small) 20mm   Pen 2 (medium) 27mm   Pen 3 (large) 35mm

The pupils, who were being individually tested and observed, were presented with all three pens in random order and asked to write their name with each pen. They were then asked to say which one was most comfortable to write with. If they were unsure they were allowed to try again, and if they were unsure after that they were allowed to choose two as being equally comfortable. The results made the children's preference quite clear.

	Pen 1	Pen 2	Pen 3	Pen 2 or 3	Pen 1 or 2
Out of 93 7-year-olds	18	53	19	3	–
Out of 100 9-year-olds	19	50	28	2	1

By secondary school the choice of pens is obviously wider. Pupils in their last year of compulsory education were asked what kind of pen they usually used for writing. Out of 104 fifteen-year-old pupils the replies were:

	Ballpoint	Rollerball	Fibre-tip	Fountain pen	Pencil
Boys	23	17	4	5	2
Girls	38	6	2	6	–
Total	61	23	6	11	2

Being cautious about drawing conclusions

It might be misleading to draw too many conclusions from these or similar statistics. Such findings might be used, for instance, to show that ballpoints are the most widely used pens, and eventually to 'prove' that ballpoints are best for secondary schools. Few of these pupils were likely to have been given a chance to experiment with a variety of pens before leaving junior school to see what might best suit their hand or their handwriting. The school was not in a very affluent area, and ballpoints are probably the cheapest and most easily available modern pens. Many of the pupils might have been using them for want of any other choice.

An entirely different picture showed up in a survey undertaken by a junior school, where pupils were given a wide choice of writing implements and helped to choose whatever suited them best. One hundred and thirteen top juniors aged mostly ten years old, were asked to list their favourite writing implement. Surprisingly a cartridge pen, with a conventional steel nib, proved to be the most popular choice. Forty-four pupils chose the traditional pen and only twenty-nine a ballpoint, while the remainder were divided between pencils and fibre- or felt-tipped pens.

Pupils of all ages may disclose details of their favourite pens, but when assessing the results, how much choice those children might have had, and how that might have influenced their decision needs to be taken into account.

16 Looking at penhold and taking pain into consideration

Over the centuries, writing masters have placed great importance on prescriptions for penhold. They were well aware of the relationship between the pen, the penhold and the resulting letters. As pens and letterforms changed, prescriptions for penhold altered too. The masters were not always in agreement about the details, and some of their recommendations look pretty strange to us today, but they worked well with the tools and in the conditions of the day. In recent years all this has been ignored. In most classrooms a variety of unconventional penholds are in evidence. At the same time modern pens are used both in the home and at school. Instead of taking the attitude that children must be at fault if they hold their pens in an unconventional way, it might be better to consider why all this has all come about.

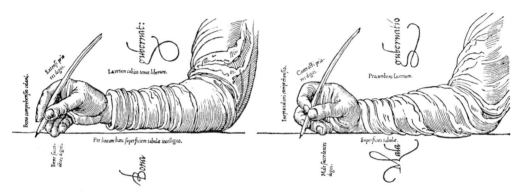

Good and bad penhold by Gerhardus Mercator, calligrapher and cartographer, 1512–94. From *Literarum Latinarum, quas Italicas Cursoriasque Vocant, Scribendarum Ratio*.

Penhold is a complicated matter, it involves so many different factors that have to be observed simultaneously: the position of the fingers, the hand position, wrist angle and so on. A way of first observing and then describing the details of penholds was needed. An analysis of penholds, reported in Sassoon, Wing and Nimmo-Smith (1986, see page 36), broke entirely new ground. Our analysis used a method of categorising the different features, so that a penhold could be described numerically and a database set up. This was a necessary step towards measuring performance, understanding why the present situation had arisen, and being able to do something about the problems of penhold today. This method is described here to assist observations of penhold. It allows the essential factors to be separated and then noted one by one. It can be used for simple observations in class and in this way leads to an understanding of how penholds with certain combinations of features, can work for one person, but not another. It is useful to photograph penholds and study them more closely, and also to video children in action. This method would allow variations in penhold, as the writer progresses across or up and down the page to be observed.

The features concerning the fingers that we tabulated were:

1. How many digits were in contact with the pen, e.g. from one to all four plus the thumb.

2. Where each digit touched the pen, e.g. at the side or the top, or right over the top as is sometimes the the case with the thumb.

3. The proximity of each digit to the pen point.

4. The angle of the joints of the digits.

The features of the hand that we tabulated were:

1. The part of the hand resting on the table – this affects the rotation of the hand.

2. The angle of the wrist – this affects whether the hand is in the inverted or non-inverted position.

3. Whether or not the wrist was supported when writing.

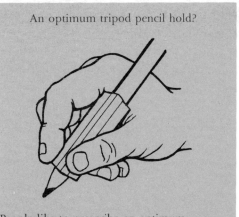

An optimum tripod pencil hold?

Different strategies for modern pens?

People like to prescribe an optimum penhold and suggest such aids as triangular pencil grips. In practice both hands and writing implements vary. Modern pens work at a different elevation to pencils, maybe we should teach different penholds for different pens.

Other factors could be added, or this method could be used in a different way. It might be interesting to look at the effects of letters with an incorrect movement, on penhold. For this it would be necessary to see the process of writing and the product at the same time. One effective way of doing this is to have a video of the pupil writing and an overhead projector reproduction of the written sample. It is then possible to locate, for example, any letters that move incorrectly upwards from the baseline, and then observe from the video how the hand has to alter direction to produce them.

It might be useful to observe and then measure the angle of the pen. This would be relatively easy to do with photographs, as would observations of how penholds might alter as the hand progresses along the line or down the page. Elaborate equipment is not needed; a hand-held camera with a fast film is good enough.

What might be discovered from observing penhold

It was observations of the angle of the pen that led me to a likely explanation of the prevalence of unconventional penholds. Modern felt- or fibre-tipped pens, and ballpoints are widely used by young children today. These pens function best at a much more upright elevation than pencils or conventional fountain pens. With the traditional penhold, the pencil is held between the thumb and the index finger at a relatively shallow angle. With a modern pen, however, the writer needs to alter the pressure of the fingers in such a way as to let the pen rise up. Several strategies can be used that modify a traditional penhold; they are worth trying as this is perhaps the quickest way to an understanding of unconventional penholds. One is to decrease the pressure from the thumb so that the index finger can exert more pressure and so let the pen become more upright. This results in the thumb no longer being in opposition to the index finger, but being moved half way over the top of the pen. Other strategies include using two or more fingers to exert extra pressure against the thumb to help the pen become more upright. Such unconventional penholds may be indications that our children are trying to develop strategies for dealing with a new generation of pens – pens that were launched without enough research into the implications of their usage. If this is so, we need to question whether the conventional tripod grip is the most appropriate penhold for the modern pens that are surely here to stay. There is an alternative penhold where the pen is held between the index and the middle finger. This allows the pen to ride up to any angle without straining the fingers. Only one pupil out of the 400 photographed in my project was found to be using this penhold, and that pupil was being forcefully persuaded to alter it by her teacher, so perhaps the lack of other examples is not so surprising. Many other children, who have spontaneously found this comfortable and effective way of dealing with modern pens, can be observed in classrooms around the world.

The artist Delacroix portrayed holding his quill between his index and middle fingers. From a French banknote.

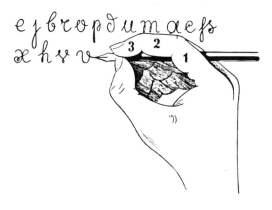

An alternative penhold illustrated by Dr H. Callewaert, a Belgian neurologist. From *L'Ecriture Rationelle* (Lebegue, 1942).

There is nothing new about this penhold. A portrait of the French artist Delacroix (1798–1863), can be found on the French 100 franc banknote. It shows the painter with his quill pen held in this way. The Belgian neurologist, Callewaert, wrote extensively about the benefits of this penhold for relieving pain and tension in patients who suffer from writer's cramp. This does not mean that we should immediately switch to teaching this penhold to all our children, but just that we should bear it in mind as an alternative to the conventional way. At the same time we should continue investigations into what is best for our pupils who will undoubtedly continue to use modern pens.

Pain

There is one important aspect of penhold that can be observed but not easily measured: that is tension. White knuckles and uncomfortably flexed joints can be useful indicators of excess pressure, and it is important that we all understand the implications. Many unconventional penholds work well, as long as the writer is relaxed, but become painful under pressure. Careful observation and questioning could lead to an understanding of why so many of our most able pupils find writing to be painful. My own research included a detailed diagnostic sheet on the subject of pain. This produced some alarming figures; forty per cent of the girls and twenty-five per cent of the boys reported that they suffered pain when writing. They also detailed such information as where exactly the pain occurred, in what particular circumstances it hurt and for how long this had been going on. Quite a few of these pupils added 'of course' when asked if writing was painful, indicating that there was often an expectation of pain.

Research into one area often reveals a surprise in another. By coincidence, the first two or three girls who reported that they suffered from pain when writing, appeared to have rather long fingers. This observation led to my taking a hand print, first of the secondary sample and subsequently of anyone else complaining of pain. It seems from the data available so far that there is some connection between pain and finger length. Other common causes of pain are likely to be tension aggravated by poor handwriting posture (including inappropriate penhold) and the increasing demand for speed in written tasks. Changing to the alternative penhold often solves the problem. It is important to remember that pain is the body's warning system and that it should not be ignored. Many writer's cramp patients can trace the origin of their trouble to some period of their lives when handwriting was painful for them. It is significant that writer's cramp is considered to be a particular problem for high achievers and perfectionists – those who typically might ignore pain when striving to reach educational or professional goals.

In a more informal situation, I recently asked the same questions about pain to a group of fifty to sixty high-achieving seventeen-year-old pupils in a girls' school in New York. Almost all the pupils in that crowded room raised their hand to indicate that it hurt them to write. If more pupils were questioned about whether they find handwriting to be painful, then teachers would soon realise the extent of this problem. They too, like the school mentioned above, might be shocked into finding methods of dealing with this problem. Detailed answers are needed from such pupils, to provide us with the information we need to help them.

17 Looking at posture and paper position

Posture and paper position are often interrelated and together they can affect penhold. It may be best to observe posture and paper position separately before drawing any conclusions from looking at both together. This may sound time-consuming but it is really very simple, and a lot can be learned in this way about how to deal with postural problems. Looking around any classroom, it is soon obvious how badly many pupils sit, and how some of them contort their bodies. These uncomfortable postures can be the result of getting used to an unsuitable paper position but there can be other causes. Inappropriate furniture, both in table and chair height, can cause young children to sit badly from the start. Strange though it might seem, children seldom alter their posture later on, even when they are supplied with appropriate furniture. Too little space on the desk or table in early years can also affect posture. Children start to write in a cramped position, and again do not always manage to make the alteration in the chain of muscle commands that would be necessary to alter their writing posture.

To tabulate the body position, at least five headings are needed, and maybe more depending on the tortured positions that individual pupils might have adopted. The most obvious are:

1. Upright

2. Leaning to the right

3. Leaning to the left

4. Bent over their work

5. Sitting sideways.

It is sometimes easier to understand and describe body posture by looking at the writer from behind. This can give a clearer picture of the strain on pupils' backs. Any information that is gained can be used to persuade the pupils of the benefits of altering their paper position so that they can sit more comfortably. Some observations may point to the fact that the classroom furniture is still inappropriate for some of the largest or smallest pupils in any group. In that case, something would have to be done before the children could be helped to deal with their postural difficulties.

Photography can be useful for verifying surveys of posture, but considerable tact is needed before showing pupils a picture of their own body. It can be quite upsetting, so it might better, wherever possible, to use a photograph of another person in a similar position to demonstrate an unusual posture.

Paper position

If children are handed a sheet of paper they will most likely place it in an almost identical position each time they commence writing. This is yet another habit that becomes automatic, and at the same time the body becomes used to fitting in with the paper position. This is beneficial providing a suitable strategy has been learned from the start,

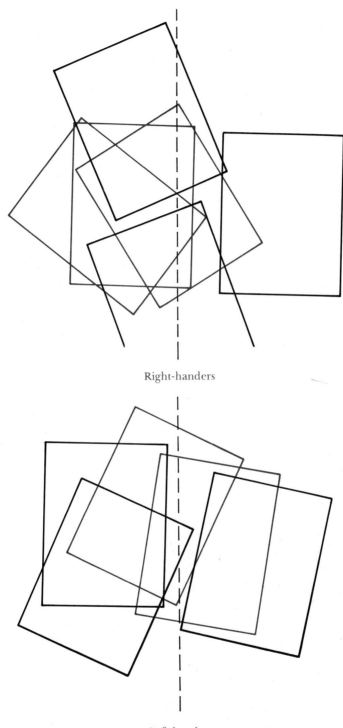

Right-handers

Left-handers

Six right- and five left-handers' paper positions are shown here, indicating at a glance how few children had found what might be considered an optimum position.

71

but the body can easily become twisted to accommodate an inappropriate paper position. This may not trouble young children very much, but later on the outcome is likely to be muscle strain and eventually pain.

The slant of the paper in relation to the edge of the table needs to be taken into consideration as well as the relation of the axis of the paper to the centre of the writer's body. An easy method of recording the necessary information follows.

When children are relaxed and writing in their normal position, place a large sheet of tracing paper over the top of their desk. Line it up to the edge of the desk and, having marked the centre of the paper, line this up to the centre of the child's body, then trace through each pupil's paper position. Several pupils' positions can be recorded on one sheet of paper. The illustrations on page 71 show how a teacher undertook a small survey on eleven of his pupils, six right-handers and five left-handers. It showed him how few of his pupils had found a paper position that would allow them to sit comfortably.

While recommending that the paper should usually be placed to the side of the writing hand, rather than centrally in front of the writer, a certain amount of flexibility is desirable within the general guidelines to accommodate different body proportions. Specific eye conditions can also affect the optimum paper position for certain children. A format rather similar to the one suggested for surveying paper position, can be useful in demonstrating to children how paper position can affect their comfort. Several different paper positions (both appropriate and inappropriate) can be marked on a sheet, then the sheet should be placed centrally before a writer. Each child can experiment by placing the paper in the pre-marked positions. Older pupils can be encouraged to try the effects of placing their paper in a complete arc. In this way they should be able to feel where it is best (and worst) for them to place their paper.

Research findings

Findings from my research, reported in Sassoon, Wing and Nimmo-Smith (1986, see page 36), showed for instance, the proportion of right- and left-handers who bent sideways because of centrally placed paper. In one school the data showed that the majority of the pupils bent closely over their work, while this was not a significant feature of the posture of pupils in the other five schools that were investigated. When this was followed up, a likely reason was soon discovered. The infant classes took place in an old-fashioned building in rooms with small, high windows. Teachers could easily be misled into thinking that lighting was adequate, but at desk level the five- and six-year-olds could not see well. They got used to bending over to see what they were doing, and a quick look at all ages showed that pupils were more than usually hunched over their work even when, later on, they had adequate lighting in more modern classrooms. Steps were taken to ensure that future intakes would not develop poor posture through inadequate lighting.

Other school surveys might be instrumental in indicating similar problems.

18 Recommendations from research into children's handwriting

It seems appropriate to present some of the general recommendations that resulted from my own research into the effects of different models and methods on how children learn to write. This project was originally undertaken as a possible advisory document for the planning of a national curriculum (Sassoon 1988, see page 36).

Many common-sense points that teachers themselves had long suspected were confirmed by the findings from this research. These can be briefly summarised:

1. The prevalence of movement faults in young children's handwriting and the effects of different models and more systematic methods of teaching in reducing such faults.

2. The variation in joining performance both within and between schools, as well as within the personal writing of some individuals.

3. The difficulties that teachers have in reproducing the school model, and the possible consequences for their pupils.

4. The wide variety of unconventional penholds.

5. The inappropriate paper position of so many children that could result in uncomfortable posture.

6. The preferred pen size when children were given a free choice.

There were some more unexpected findings too, such as the differences between the incidence of joins in boys' and girls' handwriting, and the unusual strategies developed by left-handers in their personal joins. It has not been possible to report all of it in this book, and no one survey can accurately reflect the situation nationwide.

Many of the findings pointed to a need to reconsider the use of a model. If some teachers cannot reproduce certain elements of a model, it is likely that children may find the same difficulty. Furthermore, few elements of the taught model were found in the writing of school leavers.

what will poor Robin

grandad brought my brother

These two infants are in the same class. They show how soon children develop different slant and proportion of letters.

The method is of more importance than the model

One of the main recommendations was that the emphasis of a policy should not be so much on a specific model, but more on the importance of movement. Where emphasis had been put on exit strokes and joining letters at an early age, instead of conforming to a strict model, it could be seen that there were both fewer wrongly formed letters and more joins later on. Instead of insisting on any particular model, which suggests conforming to a specific slant, proportion or possibly shape of letter, it might be more sensible to follow a systematic method of skill training which puts early emphasis on the correct movement of letters, the point of entry and direction of stroke, and on such essentials as correct height differentials. Writing habits such as penhold and paper position, must be taken into account, as well as the characteristics of modern pens. The success of any handwriting policy must surely depend on well-trained and confident teachers, so teaching handwriting should be an important part of initial as well as in-service training.

A considerable part of my research was related to joins, but at no stage has it been suggested that all letters should join, or be seen to join in children's handwriting, or later on in life for that matter. The efficiency or otherwise of what are termed 'air-joins' was, for example, not investigated. These are the movements of the pen off the paper within or between letters that necessitate repositioning of the pen. The evidence suggests however that pupils need to learn joins and then should be encouraged to use them as appropriate to their personal handwriting and the task at hand. Only when children have been helped to develop appropriate writing habits and are trained in an efficient writing movement, will it be possible to assess the degree of joining that might best lead to a fast legible handwriting. Even then, it is quite likely that the very personal and complex nature of handwriting might defy positive quantification.

> I quite like my handwriting.
> I like watching T.V. and listening to the
> my hair is brown I am medium size
> I am a very fast boy and my hobby
> And I am quite small well in other words
> My style of writing is cursive and I

Top juniors show how personal handwriting can develop with a flexible policy.

PART 3

A new way of looking at handwriting problems

However good the policy, however good the teaching, many pupils will have handwriting problems at some stage of their school life. The initial step in any diagnosis is to decide whether the pupil's condition has been the cause of the difficulties, or whether these have been caused by inadequate or inappropriate teaching.

A new perspective on handwriting problems that looks at the difficulties from the children's point of view, is needed. It would be most unfair to those children for whom handwriting may always be a problem if their plight were not discussed. In addition it must be stressed that as handwriting interacts with other skills such as spelling and grammar, deficiencies in these other areas may show through handwriting. Psychological and medical problems can also disrupt the smooth acquisition of skills.

In Part 3, some of the most usual areas of difficulty have been examined, to show how close observation and sympathetic questioning not only lead to a clearer diagnosis, but together may be the only way forward to an understanding of some of the more complex problems that afflict our children.

19 Handwriting as a diagnostic tool

The written trace is a valuable diagnostic tool. It gives a measurable and permanent indication of the writer's stage of development, and sometimes their state of mind, at any particular moment. Few children willingly have poor handwriting. Our own handwriting, for instance, may change when we are tired or tense. It may alter depending on whether we like the person we are writing to, or not, but there would be more fundamantal differences to our usual writing if real problems were involved. Supposing we had an accident and had to learn to write with our non-preferred hand; supposing we developed an illness that left us with a tremor; or supposing we suffered a nervous breakdown, would we expect our handwriting to remain unchanged? Of course not, so we should realise that the writing of children who may be suffering from any of a wide variety of conditions, will reflect these conditions. In the classroom they are often expected to be able to attain the same level of handwriting as pupils with no similar problems. If we could look at handwriting problems as an indicator and a diagnostic tool instead of measuring problem handwriting against some mythical norm, this would be a positive and major step forward.

Schools may be accustomed to accepting that children termed 'clumsy' may never excel at gymnastics or games, even after the therapy that such children deserve to receive. If these children's motor co-ordination is such that they find difficulty, for example, in catching a ball, then this awkwardness will quite likely be reflected in their handwriting. They may never be able to produce the neat, conventional handwriting that some teachers expect to be presented with. Awkward hands are likely to produce awkward handwriting, so children should not be castigated for conditions over which they have little control. If they are nagged for producing 'untidy' written work, then tension will be added to their natural clumsiness. This will only exacerbate the situation. Of course, any practical advice that might assist the writer, especially in the way of changes in writing posture, should be proffered. Apart from that, providing the handwriting is legible and fast enough for the writer to keep up in class, surely those children deserve praise for the way they are tackling a job that is more difficult for them than for others. A positive attitude is most likely to relax the writer. The relaxation will probably be reflected in the written work, and any resulting praise will help to improve the self-image of these unfortunate children who daily have to see their best efforts condemned as untidy.

Co-ordination problems

The word 'dyspraxic' is increasingly used to describe those with co-ordination problems. This term suggests that the problem may lie with the organisation of the sequencing of commands needed for any complex movement. Handwriting, as well as everyday tasks, becomes problematic, and special techniques are needed to address the central issue of how best to equip such children with a strategy for developing their own strategies. These children profit from each task being broken down into simpler sections. These simplified tasks then need to be repeated several times. At each stage, some kind of personal reminder should be included in the teaching process. This could be in the form of a rhyme, a picture, or a pattern, whichever appeals to the individual.

Any teaching or remedial technique needs to take into account the different ways that children may best assimilate information. As far as handwriting is concerned, whereas many children can learn visually, some may need a more kinaesthetic approach, and a few children may only be able to learn from an oral description of any movements involved. It is essential to identify the best approach for those with problems. If children have failed to profit from class teaching when others have succeeded, the answer could be something as simple as a completely different approach to the subject. By watching such children carefully, it is usually clear when they have finally understood. Whichever technique is successful, it may be used to help in other areas of learning too. Finding a way to explain handwriting to a child can sometimes lead to the solving of other problems.

20 Problems that show through handwriting

As other cognitive skills interact with handwriting, a problem with other areas of learning may show through handwriting. If pupils have difficulty with spelling, for example, they may hesitate before or in the middle of words and in doing so disrupt the flow of their handwriting. At best, the writing of a bad speller may look uneven and somewhat disjointed. If children are still writing in pencil and try to erase their errors, their work will look messy and invite criticism. If they are using ink, then constant crossing out may make an even more unattractive page. So pupils may be criticised for untidiness or poor presentation but often this is nothing to do with how well they can form letters. The untidiness is a direct result of not being able to spell.

Another reason why poor spellers' handwriting may appear difficult to read concerns the way adults scan and read words. If part of a word is omitted as a result of spelling errors, or inappropriate letters substituted, then the shape of the word may be so distorted that the reader might claim that the writing is illegible.

As children grow older and become more aware of their shortcomings, then tension will increase as they prepare themselves to face undeserved criticism of their 'handwriting'. They may know that when they are copying out a familiar sentence their handwriting is as good as anyone else's. The frustration that can arise from the injustice of such criticism will certainly not help to cure any underlying spelling fault. When impartial adults look deeper, they might find that while some children will always have trouble with spelling, others may well never have been taught how to spell. Once again, they are being unjustly blamed for shortcomings in the educational system.

It is quite easy to separate spelling from the formation of letters in order to pinpoint this kind of problem. You can give a child a repetitive letter exercise that does not involve any

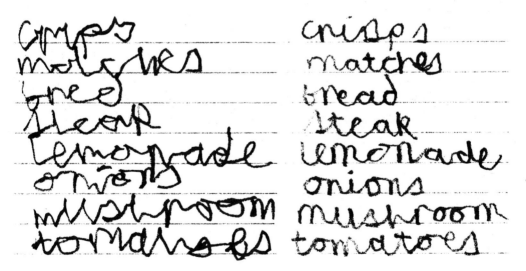

When this boy is given a spelling test his worries are reflected in the handwriting. When copying corrections, most of the signs of tension have disappeared.

spelling. If the letters are well formed and consistent, it is likely that the problem does not lie with the handwriting itself but that there is another problem showing through it.

Such understanding may not have 'cured' anything, but the teacher now has a clearer idea of where the trouble lies, and the pupils have the comfort of showing that at least their handwriting, in terms of letterforms, is satisfactory.

Psychological problems reflected in handwriting

Psychological problems of all kinds are likely to be reflected in handwriting. These indications can be recognised by the informed observer and used as a way of understanding the writer's state of mind. The causes of tension obviously vary considerably. With children, bereavement for example, or bullying, a new baby, a broken home caused by divorce or any of these alone or in combination, can be so upsetting as to disrupt what was a perfectly adequate handwriting. The effect of such tension can compound any other difficulties the child might have.

Tension can affect handwriting in various ways and these differences quickly become evident. It may be useful for diagnostic purposes to imagine the hand that could produce such tortured letters. Perhaps the most unhappy pages of handwriting are those that present great variability. It suggests such a waste of potential when some passages are written in a mature hand, while others appear jagged with tension, or so uncontrolled as to be illegible. Some of the most important clues to children's problems, reflected through their handwriting, come from comparing their best letters with their worst.

The tense uneven handwriting of a left-hander diagnosed as having grapho-motor problems. Under pressure of speed it becomes illegible. Keyboards can provide relief in such cases.

21 Specific problems for left-handers

The section in this book on planning a policy suggests that provision should be made for left-handers. This kind of provision would mean that care should be taken in lighting, seating and writing implements, and allowance made for space for paper to be placed to the left side of the writer.

There are usually other factors that need to be understood about most left-handers and some things that need to be understood about a minority with real problems. The first point to be grasped concerns the 'look' of left-handed handwriting; the initial impression may be that it slopes backwards. Some people dislike the look of backward-sloping writing, and seem to think that it implies some kind of weakness of character. As far as young left-handed children are concerned, the slant is a direct result of writing with a conventional penhold and hand position. This is an interesting experiment to try for oneself; take a pencil in either hand and make a pattern of diagonal strokes. For the right-hander, the strokes will probably slope forward. With the left hand, the diagonal usually slopes backwards. To be sure of a forward-slanting line many young left-handers have to invert their hand position, that means twisting their wrist to write from above the line of writing. Many left-handers manage to alter the slant of their letters in later life without inverting, but young children may not be able to do this manipulation of their fingers when they are just learning to write.

In some countries, the national model slopes forward. A forward slant is enforced still in many parts of the United States; indeed paper with a forward-slanting grid is sometimes used to teach the first stages of cursive. Maybe this is the reason why so many Americans use an inverted penhold, and why their research sometimes tries to justify this penhold on neurological grounds. In Great Britain, despite remarks about the appearance of a backward slant, the forward slant is seldom enforced, and there also appears to be less incidence of inverted penhold. My own research revealed only one inverted writer at the age of 15+ and none in the younger age groups. Closer questioning and testing of the sixteen (out of 100) left-handed pupils in the 15+ group revealed (in a test that was meant for quite a different purpose) that at least four of them (twenty-five per cent) had changed spontaneously from an inverted or semi-inverted posture at some time during their secondary schooling. The pupils reported that this was because they had found the inverted posture either painful or too slow. The relaxed policy on handwriting in Great Britain has some benefits. It allows us to observe those who are inclined to experiment with different writing postures, and to learn from their individual solutions. It is tempting to draw conclusions from what we observe, but much harder to assess what the results would be if we helped children to find suitable strategies for themselves at an early age.

Spacing

The informed observer can often detect the effects of poor writing posture through left-handers' writing. Spacing may present a problem if the left hand obscures whatever has just been written. Children who space their separate letters unusually widely may be indicating that they need guidance in altering their paper position so that they can see

kee P th at book t idy

This young left-hander obscured his writing so he could not space his letters well.

what they are doing. A more involved situation arises when children have taken the teaching of joins too literally and join so much that their letters become distorted. The left-handed action often involves more pushing than is desirable for a relaxed handwriting. It may be easy to explain that more penlifts will result in a more relaxed writing, but it can be difficult for writers to unjoin letters and then space them closely enough in a word. To writers who have been joining all their letters within every word, a penlift has usually been accompanied by lateral movement sufficient to produce a word space. A careful demonstration might be needed in these circumstances. This could show how the hand should follow exactly the same path that it would in the case of a join, only the pen is lifted and then repositioned. Adults produce all the actions of writing automatically and tend to forget the intermediate movements that are involved. It may be necessary to analyse each separate action that takes place, then the sequence can be explained to children to help them to overcome their problems.

Right or left: a difficult decision

Being right-handed or left-handed is not a clear cut issue: it is more of a continuum. Some people seem to be more definitely right- or left-handed than others and a few are ambidextrous. It may be advantageous for a tennis player to be ambidextrous but it is becoming apparent that this may not be helpful in handwriting. If a child has no hand preference a teacher or parent may step in and make a decision. If no decision is made and a child is left to alternate between hands, then neither hand, so the argument goes, will get sufficiently practised. More often than not the right hand will be chosen, but no-one will know if the correct decision has been taken for several years and by then it may be too late to rectify a mistake.

'When I was seven the teacher, when she saw that the left-handers were messy, told us that all the left-handers should write right-handed. I changed and now I can only write slowly. When there is a word that I find hard and I stop to think how to spell it, I get all lost.'

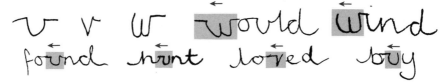

The boy whose quote appears above, formed many of his letters from right to left. Although it was almost unnoticeable on the page, this slowed him down considerably.

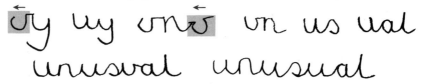

80

There are a variety of tests to help to find a child's preferred hand, which are usually based on a battery of precision tasks including threading, tracking and dotting. It is usually necessary to look closely at how the arm, wrist and fingers of each hand function. The hand should be observed when it is supported and while writing. A pattern task is not always sufficient as children may use a drawing strategy for pattern instead of a writing one, and a drawing strategy does not require a supported hand. A comparison of the line quality produced by each hand is sometimes a help, but a trained eye is needed to detect the variations.

If there are no definite clues to a writer's preferred hand then the decision is best left with the child. First of all children should be made aware of the issues involved. They may have no idea of the desirability of the predominant use of one hand. Once alerted, experimentation may then be the best way for children to make up their own minds. Talking to the many unfortunate pupils for whom the wrong decision has been taken, it is clear that it is not only their letters that have been affected.

The consequences that may arise from a wrong decision

A few cases might help to illustrate, from the pupils' angle, how an incorrect decision might affect them. The subject is so complex, that these cases should not be taken as a basis for any theoretical rules. They are purely anecdotal and are presented as illustrations of the need to listen to children in trouble and try to understand their difficulties – and to learn from them.

Case 1

The wrong choice of hand had serious consequences for a young teenager. He had been referred because of a history of learning difficulties and behavioural problems. His therapist had become convinced that the boy should have been left-handed not right-handed and asked for advice. It was not even necessary to give the boy any of the usual graphic tests, as he volunteered in general conversation that although he usually wrote, as he had been taught to do, with his right hand, he had always wondered why he could think more clearly on the occasions that he used his left hand. When pressed further he explained in very simple words what few people even theorise about; when he wrote with his right hand there always seemed to be a delay between his deciding what to write, and his hand getting it on to the page. It was then possible to explain in the simplest of neurological terms why this should happen. His 'delay' was most likely the result of using the wrong hand. Once the boy had a logical explanation of at least part of his trouble and the resulting frustration, his behavioral problems cleared up. When last heard of he still had not the confidence to train his left hand to write all the time, but that should come with time.

Case 2

This concerns a boy for whom the wrong decision had been made in infant school. He was first interviewed at about the age of nine. The boy himself was quite sure that he preferred to write with his left hand, and also described without prompting that when he 'wanted to work anything out' he needed to use his left hand. The decision was made, despite considerable antagonism from the school, that the boy should be allowed to use his left hand. It was a struggle at first as the left hand had not been as practised as the right one, so the handwriting appeared to deteriorate. Some five years later it is still possible to trace this boy's learning difficulties to the initial incorrect decision. His handwriting varies from being mature to uncontrolled and illegible, and often mirrors his inner tensions. He is articulate and intelligent, but a reluctant writer. Because of this he is underachieving in many areas of his work. Rightly or wrongly he still blames his negative attitude to writing to his early frustration and the confusion over which hand to use.

The visual aspect needs also to be understood, because in certain cases it can play a part in a decision about handedness. It is not essential that the leading eye and the preferred hand should be on the same side. It is quite common for these two to differ and the resulting condition, known as cross laterality, usually sorts itself out without intervention. Two problems might arise: firstly, if a child has no leading eye as well as no preferred hand; and secondly when a child has a strong leading eye connected with the preferred hand, but the incorrect hand has been chosen for writing. It is now well known that a leading eye needs to be established for the sake of scanning both in reading and writing, and this can usually be done by means of simple orthoptic exercises.

When the decision is made to strengthen one eye it is important to be sure that the preferred hand has been correctly chosen. The following case illustrates what might happen if the wrong decision is taken.

Case 3

A seventeen-year-old boy asked why he could only write with his head flat on the table and leaning on his right side. He said that if he sat upright everything looked blurred. The first suggestion made was that perhaps he was left-handed and right-eyed. He replied that someone had suggested that he was left-handed and his parents had taken this up and trained him from an early age to use his left hand for everything. Gradually he came to the conclusion that he was not left-handed after all, and now used his right hand for everything except handwriting. What should he do? If he was naturally right-handed and right-eyed it might not be advisable, or even possible, to strengthen his left eye so that he could sit up straight to write. (By leaning his head on the right side he was self-occluding his right eye.) If he went on writing in this position he would end up with backache. This was already becoming a considerable problem, but school-leaving examinations were looming and he was not at all practised with his right hand. The only advice that could be given was to get over his examinations and then see if he could slowly retrain himself, by practising with his right hand. He would need to remember to alter his paper position to suit both hand and eye, and expect that the resulting handwriting might look different from that written by his left hand. A word processor would probably be a help with lengthy writing tasks in the transitional period, and also be quite appropriate for him as a student.

Other left-handers' troubles include those caused by the left-to-right movement of our alphabet. These are dealt with in the following section on directionality.

22 Problems with directionality

Handwriting is a taught skill whose conventions vary from culture to culture. In our culture the direction of writing is from top to bottom and from left to right. This movement needs to be practised at the pre-writing stage and reinforced for those who indicate that they may be having difficulty in this area. Maybe this subject needs to be looked at in a wider sense and the problems of children struggling with directionality in writing systems that work in directions different to our own should be examined. This book must confine itself to dealing with problems resulting from a left-to-right movement, but while doing so we must not forget the possible difficulties of children in our schools who may be having to deal with two writing systems and two different directions of writing simultaneously.

The problem of directionality is seldom mentioned in books about handwriting, and not easily understood by those who have never been bothered themselves by such a difficulty. It is not even readily understood by those who are affected, so it needs as clear an explanation as possible. Take a pencil and draw a short line from left to right and then one from right to left. It is likely that one direction will be easier for you than the other.

Which direction is easier for you?

If you are right-handed the left-to-right line usually is best. If you are left-handed then the right-to-left direction will probably be easiest for you. This matter of directionality and how it relates to the preferred hand has been quantified by those concerned in forensic document examination, and may be useful in detecting forgeries. Directionality problems, however, need to be related here to what happens in ordinary handwriting.

Some left-handers have more trouble than others with the left-to-right direction of writing. This might be the result of some children having less left-to-right orientation training at the pre-writing and early handwriting stages. The problem is likely to be worse for those who were meant to be right-handed but have to write with their non-preferred hand after an accident or some other damage to their right side. Whatever the cause of such difficulties the children concerned need understanding and informed help. Some examples of particular difficulties and solutions are given here.

Case 1
This concerns a young boy who had lost the use of his right hand but had managed to write quite well with his left until it became time to join up his letters. This was not a simple case of clockwise 'o's, but a discernable difficulty in the left-to-right movement needed to proceed smoothly from letter to letter. For this boy, who was obviously right-handed but could no longer use his preferred hand, something needed to be done to help him internalise the left-to-right flow of joined letters. It seemed to help him if he motioned the movement with his damaged right hand. In some way the knowledge of this movement transferred and helped him to start to get some flow into his letters.

Observing direction

Evidence of preferred direction can be observed in the way people cross their letter 't' and perhaps 'f'. Crossing a separate letter is one step, joining to the next letter is another. A right-hander may choose, consciously or unconsciously from a variety of what are termed 'crossbar joins' to speed up the joining from 't' or 'f'. A left-hander who may automatically cross from right to left is less likely to benefit from such short cuts. This may not be a great disadvantage; it may assume greater importance to the observer of the movement of handwriting than to the writer.

It is difficult to assess how prevalent serious directional problems are since they are seldom recognised. Some pupils devise techniques themselves with varying success, while others collect such labels as 'slow writer' or 'cannot join up'.

Case 2

This boy's case illustrates the need for a new way of looking at handwriting that would observe and then take such complex problems into consideration. Aged about eleven, the boy was referred by his teacher because his handwriting was 'untidy'. The boy's explanation was illuminating. He was left-handed and demonstrated what happened when he wrote slowly enough to satisfy the teacher on 'neatness' grounds. He got muddled in the middle of some letters, retracing them in a clockwise direction. When he moved slowly from letter to letter, the confusion was more pronounced as he struggled against the desire to go from right to left. However he had discovered that if he wrote fast enough he could overcome both his strong right-to-left pull and clockwise movement, but then his teacher criticised the faster writing for being untidy. The frustration of such pupils must sometimes be so great that behavioural problems would not be surprising. A letter to the teacher explained the boy's predicament, and the way he was trying to solve a tricky problem. Similar confrontations could be avoided if it were generally realised that left-handers may have directional problems. A discussion might help both pupil and teacher to understand the difficulty and work out a compromise.

Case 3

A left-handed boy in another school gave a further insight into directionality problems. His report said 'slow at handwriting, never gets enough down in class'. That description might indicate anything from the pupil being a bad speller to being an 'awkward' left-hander with co-ordination problems. It might also indicate a visual problem which would be a distinct disadvantage in the boy's school where far too much of the teaching seemed to consist of pupils copying notes from the blackboard. Hand and eye are used together in handwriting, and it is possible that directionality could affect scanning as well as the act of writing.

In order to test whether spelling was at the heart of this boy's problem, several complicated words were written on the blackboard. He memorised the first portion of a word and wrote it down with no difficulty, but when he looked up at the board and started to write the second half of the word, his problem was obvious. It was as if a magnet were pulling his hand from right to left, so strong was his right-to-left directionality. It needed a conscious effort to set the writing in motion in a left-to-right direction. If this happened each time he looked up in the middle of a word, it was not surprising that he was slow at copying from the board. When the boy was tested in a different way by dictating several sentences to him at speed, he had no trouble in keeping up. There was no easy answer to this problem which occurred more when he was scanning and copying long words than when he was writing spontaneously, but it was at least a relief to the boy that his problem was understood. Further solutions might include being allowed to use a friend's notes to supplement his own, and the use of a word processor for other written tasks.

Right-handers may be affected too

How many other children have undiagnosed directional problems and are instead labelled slow, or stupid? They may not realise in what way they are slightly different from their friends. There may be little that can be done, specially if such problems have remained undiagnosed for years, but the least that these children deserve is praise for their resourcefulness in trying to work things out for themselves.

Case 4

This case demonstrates that directional 'differences' or preferences are not confined to the left-to-right movement or to left-handers. A right-handed girl aged about eight years old was referred, supposedly for an unusual penhold. Indeed she did use a technique that involved pushing with her thumb but that was not her real problem. The piece of writing that she brought gave no clue either; its only unusual feature was that each line was written in a different colour; so colour seemed a good tool to use to get this nervous child to relax. When given a choice of coloured pens she seemed unusually hesitant but reacted positively when told that she could use a different one for every letter if she wanted to. At that she started to write something in the bottom right-hand corner that eventually emerged as her name written from bottom to top. When the first example was met with approval she happily reproduced this several times. When tested with a spiral pattern it could be seen that bottom to top was her preferred direction. Writing in that unusual direction resulted in the trace with best line quality. When asked to write in the conventional direction she immediately complained of tiredness and it was obvious that it was a considerable strain for her to maintain a left-to-right and top-to-bottom direction. The immediate future would not be easy for this child, but at least her problem had been recognised. Exercises to encourage a conventional movement should eventually help her, but until then allowance would have to be made for the fact that writing might be quite a strain.

This child's unusual problem was discovered almost by accident. She was caught off her guard so allowed it to show through her writing. In class she would probably struggle to write conventionally. If we do not discover their particular difficulty, such children may go through life without any help, and with an inaccurate and potentially damaging label attached to them. Those who are labelled 'dyslexic' or some other such term, resent this when they know themselves that this is not the case.

23 Perceptual problems

It is not always easy to differentiate between directional and perceptual problems when using handwriting alone as a diagnostic tool, but when faced with vague diagnoses that do not seem to explain why a particular child should have handwriting difficulties, any clue should be investigated. Sometimes complex perceptual problems may be detected by watching the writer in action as much as through the actual handwriting. There may be little that can be done to accelerate the body's own way of accommodating these unusual conditions, but once the problem is identified, at least such children may get the sympathy they deserve while they come to terms with their difficulties. It is impossible to tell how many children have perceptual problems as they do not necessarily know that they see things in a different way from others. These pupils may be labelled slow or 'dyslexic' or some other inadequate description, and suffer from the consquences.

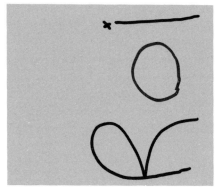

A right-hander's preferred direction was bottom to top.

S!

This boy reads best upside-down, and has difficulty in remembering which way up to write his letters. He invented an exercise to help anyone else in the same predicament to tell the difference between 'n' and 'u' – a pattern showing 'u' under 'n'.

Case 1

A bright-eyed boy aged about nine stood out in a group of children who were supposed to have severe learning difficulties, because of his self-confidence – a characteristic that was sadly lacking in all the others. We were sitting at a table near a window while an excavator was at work outside in the school grounds. Neither of us could resist watching it from time to time, and this proved most valuable. The boy was in the middle of writing the word 'six' when he suddenly produced the letter 'i' upside down with the dot on the baseline. He was about to rub this out when I stopped him and started asking questions such as: 'Does this happen often?' 'What does your teacher say?' His answers showed exactly how he had worked out ways of dealing with his own problem: 'It does not happen as often as it used to. The teacher does not know about it as I always rub out the upside-down letters. She is always saying that my work is messy because it has so many rubbed-out letters' were some of his replies. The answer to the question 'When does it happen most often?', produced another accurate and intelligent explanation: 'When there is something interesting happening in the room and I look up and then down again at my work'. In other words whenever his concentration is broken. Instead of being able to automate his handwriting and forget about the formation of letters like most other children of his own age, this boy would need to think consciously about each letter as he writes. In answer to the question 'Have you any suggestions for other young children with the same problem as you?', this amazing boy gave a precise answer. He said that the most difficult pair of letters were 'u' and 'n'. He still had trouble trying to remember whether he had corrected them or not. Together we worked out several ideas that might help with that particular discrimination.

This boy's problem should eventually disappear, but in the meantime he needs understanding, and above all less criticism if there are rubbings out, or if he takes a little longer to finish his work. He had a computer at home and enjoyed using it. It might be a good idea to allow him to use it as a word processor for some of his homework. One of the risks for children who write slowly, for whatever reason, is that unless they meet with understanding, they may just reduce the amount of written work that they produce. Another boy aged nine or ten with similar problems reported that sometimes he sat up until nearly midnight to complete his homework. This was his, not very satisfactory, solution to the frustration of slow handwriting.

Case 2

This five-year-old girl's case shows how, if some perceptual problems are diagnosed early enough, a structured method and supportive, repetitive teaching can help to solve them. This is best demonstrated through a series of illustrations that show how the child had no perception of letters at the stage, during the first year at school, when most of her peers could write their own names. After considerable systematic teaching of the movement of letters, when many of the class were already beginning to join their letters, she started to copy letters. At that stage she displayed a variety of unusual reversals that suggested possible perceptual difficulties. At no time was this child tested in any formal way to discover what her specific problems could be. In her district this would be unlikely before the age of seven. The teacher of this class of thirty children was introducing into her school a systematic method similar to the one suggested in this book. All she did was to ensure that this girl was encouraged to repeat each stage of the system of letter and word exercises until she had assimilated each one. At the end of the year this child could write simple words with all the letters moving correctly. This seemed just as much of a justification of the system as the excellent flowing handwriting that the other children were producing.

(am 5)

These reversals were sorted out in the first year by a systematic method of teaching movement.

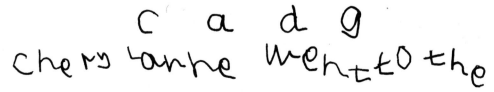

Visual problems

Severe visual problems can distort and disrupt pupils' performance not only in handwriting but in many other areas, resulting in needless misery and waste of potential. Ordinary tests do not necessarily detect such complications, but it is sometimes possible, without being an expert, to suspect an eye problem from some hint from the writer or suspicion of an unusual posture. A particular teenager in such a situation wrote a poignant letter of thanks. She had been labelled 'awkward, slow and stupid', and indeed her whole body posture suggested dejection and misery. A clue to her difficulty came from noticing that her eyes did not appear to be focussing on her work, and that she held her head at an unusual angle to write. Her story of different schools in various countries may have meant that the usual health checks had not been carried out. Once glasses had been prescribed, for what admittedly turned out to be a complicated condition, her whole attitude to life and work changed. She wrote and thanked, but the saddest part of the letter read 'how different my life would have been if this had been discovered earlier'. Such cases may not be very common. An awareness of such possibilities may result in a few needless visits to an orthoptist or other specialist, but for some children this might be the key to solving their problems. These cases are in addition to the more common problem of having no leading eye. Orthoptic tests are recommended for children with reading or writing problems since it has been shown that without a leading eye some children may encounter specific difficulties.

Occasionally difficulties that appear to be caused by complex visual or perceptual problems may have relatively simple solutions. A child had been tested and was reported to have unusual problems causing him to perceive and produce figures asymmetrically. This case demonstrates how misleading such reports can be in certain circumstances. The child, a cerebral palsy patient, had poor posture for a variety of reasons, and tended to sit somewhat sideways to the table. In addition he had an uncorrected squint. When asked to draw his mother who was sitting opposite him, the picture was indeed lopsided, but by observing the child in action it was obvious that he was turning his head even more sideways than his awkward posture demanded. The most likely cause would be that he was attempting to occlude his left eye, the one with the squint, and use only the right one for drawing or writing. When the paper was moved well over to the child's right side (he was right-handed) so that he could see what he was doing while using only his right eye, not only did his entire posture improve, but his drawings were absolutely symmetrical. Such a simple but practical solution may not often arise, but we must always ensure that all children are in the optimum writing position for their particular situation. Only when such practical steps have been taken is it possible to make the accurate assessment that is essential in order to plan a remedial programme.

24 Observing, assessing and dealing with tremors

Tremors can arise from a variety of causes. Some are curable or at least containable but others are progressive. The level of tremor needs first to be assessed through a close observation of the writer and the written trace, then practical help can be given to minimise the effects of the tremor. Occasionally a slight tremor may be the result of tension. A boy showed signs of a tremor through his early letters when entering the reception class but it had completely disappeared by the end of the first year at school. He was in the same class as the young girl with perceptual problems, mentioned in the last section. Undoubtedly the school's encouraging, confident, systematic method helped the boy concerned, and by the end of the year his writing was relaxed, flowing and tremor-free. In his case parental pressure might have been the cause. Certainly too much pressure from either home or school may affect some children in this way at almost any time in their school life, and it may not always be easy to differentiate between a tension tremor and one caused by more serious conditions.

Cerebral palsy

Mild cerebral palsy is one of the commonest causes of tremor in children in mainstream schools. If their condition is severe enough children will usually receive special education from the start, and be given appropriate keyboard training to minimise the disadvantages that a tremor might pose for handwritten communication.

Case 1
This illustrates how some children can slip through the net. This ten-year-old girl illustrates how a tremor may to a certain extent respond to remedial help, but eventually an assessment may be needed to ensure that the handwriting is adequate for secondary school work. Her situation was somewhat unusual as she was profoundly deaf, so was in a unit that dealt with that problem rather than with her other physical handicaps.

A quick 'test' showed that the tremor affected most of her directional strokes. She was asked to draw a picture of a house; this made it easy to judge the degree of tremor without making her aware of being tested. Formal testing may make children tense and so give a distorted picture of their everyday performance.

When the girl was first seen, she was writing with her head flat on the desk and her left hand tipped over in such a way that she could not see what she had written. Everything was done to improve her writing posture. Her physiotherapist helped her to improve her seated posture and a slanting board was made for her. This gave more support for her extended arm and controlled the tremor to a certain extent. The special material that ensured a resilient writing surface had the added advantage of being non-slip. Where this is not available a pad of newspaper would do almost as well. All this gave her a better chance of writing and it certainly cured the original hand position, but there were still considerable difficulties. In the end a word processor was recommended, just in time for this girl to prepare for the written tasks expected in secondary school.

Before

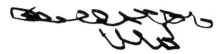

Joins help.

A simple test to show tremor.

A slanting board and then a suitable paper position helped. Notice the change of penhold.

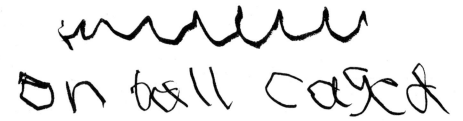

The tremor was still too severe to allow this girl to write well enough for secondary school (as the examples above show). She needed, and got a keyboard.

Case 2

This case illustrates how a tremor can occur quite suddenly and become a major problem for a teenager. This particular boy had been considered somewhat clumsy but nothing more. He was highly intelligent and just about to embark on examinations when a more serious condition became evident involving a considerable tremor. A word processor was the obvious choice for him, but this created another difficulty. He had no experience of using a keyboard and it would take him some time to get up enough speed to find it of much practical use. An interim strategy was needed. His school had put the boy back on to separate letters, but the constant repositioning of the pen only accentuated the difficulties caused by the tremor. First he needed a strategy for steadying his hand as much as possible. He rejected a slanted desk, saying that he had already tried it but had not found it helpful. Perhaps inadequate advice at the same time on other aspects of handwriting had failed to give him confidence in whoever was trying to help him. His confidence was regained when we experimented with both a slant and techniques for using his non-writing hand to steady the one that he was using to write.

A task appropriate to his age – drawing a square with opposing corners joined to test diagonals – revealed that his horizontal strokes were less affected by the tremor than the others. In such cases it is sometimes possible to modify letters and joins to maximise the use of strokes that are least affected by the tremor. The following illustrations show how successful this was. Perhaps this would be enough to stop this boy from falling too far behind with his work while he developed his keyboard skills.

Both these cases highlight the benefits of teaching keyboard skills at as early a stage as possible to those who might need them. This should not be used as an excuse to stop writing altogether, but as a help when handwriting, for whatever reason, is not adequate for certain tasks.

Separate letters may make a tremor more noticeable because repositioning the pen is difficult.

Horizontal joins helped minimise the effects of this tremor. A word processor was better still.

25 Fatigue

Handwriting can occasionally help to solve a problem that has defied the accurate diagnosis needed to plan remedial strategies.

Case 1

This involved a six-year-old boy who had suffered a rare condition from birth but who had responded sufficiently well to treatment to be able to attend mainstream school. A handwriting sample provided a clue that surprised his parents and teachers as well as the team of therapists that dealt with this interesting case. The report said that although the boy had a reading age several years above his age, his letters appeared all over the page, with no organisation or control. Further questioning of the parents revealed that the child had been immobile for much of his first two years and showed difficulty in recognising scale models of everyday items. This brought up the possibility of sensory deprivation. This term is used to describe the condition of those who may have missed out the vital stages of early development, when a baby discovers its own body and begins to explore its relationship with the outside world. In the long term this child may need skilled therapy to offset his early disabilities but in the short term it was his handwriting that needed investigating.

It was arranged to see the boy at his home, so he returned from school after his lunch-time rest period. The parents were asked to provide a sample of his handwriting, so they had asked the boy to write a simple sentence before he left for school that day. Neither the previously written sentence, nor the simple graphic exercises that the boy produced for me that afternoon revealed a particularly serious state of affairs. The sample that he had written before leaving for school was of a good standard for a child of his age.

A meeting had been arranged with his teachers and the therapists dealing with the case later that afternoon. A sample that the boy had written at school was produced and this revealed quite a different picture; a series of uncontrolled quavery marks on a page.

The reason for these differences were eventually explained by looking at the different writing situations. The boy wore heavy callipers, but the teachers said that he was highly competitive and tried to do everything that his able-bodied friends did. He was provided with a personal tutor for the second half of each morning but very little progress was made as he was not co-operative. His behaviour at lunch-time was causing concern, but the period after the lunch-time rest period usually went better. Looking at this problem as an outsider it became obvious that the differences in handwriting as well as the behavioural problems could be due to fatigue, and this proved to be the case. Once his day was reorganised to make the best use of the times when he was least tired, life became easier for everyone. He was encouraged to write at home when he was more relaxed, and his tutor arranged to come either early in the morning or after his lunch-time rest period.

This case illustrates the possible effect that fatigue might have on the performance of physically handicapped children, when competing against able-bodied children in mainstream schools. It also shows how we must be able to ask and answer the necessary questions if the children are too young to understand or answer for themselves.

Case 2

This case involved either fatigue or perhaps malaise. It occurred in a small town in Australia where a ten-year-old girl was taught in a special group because of her supposed learning difficulties. The teacher supplied one vital clue when she said that the child was difficult to deal with because she varied so much from day to day. Not only did her handwriting vary wildly but on her 'dreamy days' she seemed jumpy when anyone approached her. This immediately suggested a medical condition rather than a learning difficulty.

Inevitably, when the girl came to see me after school there was nothing wrong with the handwriting that she produced, but the answer to my first question surprised her mother. In reply to the question 'Do you know when you get up in the morning whether you are going to have a good day or a bad day?', the girl smiled broadly and said 'of course'. No-one had ever thought to ask her such a question before and she had accepted the label of being a problem at school and never tried to explain how she felt.

The mother then provided several possible explanations: first the girl had suffered an attack of whooping cough several years earlier and had missed a whole term of school at an important stage of development. Not only would there be problems for her because she had lost so much basic learning, but it would be likely that for some time after such a severe illness she would not be well enough to assimilate much during school hours. This would not be taking into account any possible brain damage that might have occurred in an attack of whooping cough severe enough to last for three months. A question to the mother about possible allergies that might contribute to her daughter's 'dreamy' condition, revealed that allergies to colourants and additives had been identified but the family had problems organising a diet that excluded such food. How this was all connected, and what could be done to help this unfortunate child needed to be carefully worked out under medical supervision. All that I could do on a flying visit to that town was to suggest that the family should keep a diary that recorded good days, bad days, diet and any other possible causes.

Considering the effects of fatigue

We have no way of knowing how many more children are wrongly labelled because of such conditions. We need to be aware of the possibility without over-reacting, realising that the person who holds the vital clue is often the pupil. Perhaps the effects of fatigue should be more widely taken into consideration. Fatigue will often show through handwriting and can affect the way children are judged. This could be relevant to those who may be less physically mature than others of their peers, or to many teenagers for whom fatigue is often the normal condition.

26 Gaps in learning

Children who have missed a period of schooling may pose particular and hidden problems in the classroom. If the cause was serious illness, then it is to be hoped that this will appear on their record when they move from school to school. If however they have attended school but for whatever reason have not been in a state to take in the teaching from which other children have profited, then this might not be so readily recorded. One category of such children are those suffering from allergies, in particular those that cause hyperactivity. If they have been lucky enough to have been diagnosed early, and a satisfactory dietary regime has been established, then by the time they reach junior school there may be no evidence of their previous disorder. If the disorder had resulted in wild and maybe antisocial behaviour, then it is understandable that parents might want to forget that period. They may not wish to pass on such information to a new school. But is this fair to the children? Through no real fault of their own, it is unlikely that much of the first two years of teaching would have been absorbed. A hyperactive child does not sit still or concentrate for many minutes at a time. As far as handwriting is concerned such children may have not taken in much of the essential grounding. At the age that other children are ready to join up their letters, having automated many aspects of handwriting, children who took little in during the first year or two will be at a distinct disadvantage. They may have no strategies for organising the movement of letters and may need to be taken right back to basics. This will not be easy in a busy junior classroom.

Confusion over basic aspects of handwriting is common to those children who have had to move home and therefore school, several times in the early years. It may affect those for whom English is a second language and who might have found it difficult to comprehend instructions when younger, though they are competent English speakers by the time they reach junior school. Children who have had strong medication in early school days may also have found it difficult to concentrate and take much in. What about such relatively common conditions as meningitis or encephalitis? It may take months or even years before the patient is restored to full health; in the meantime headaches and fatigue may interfere with all aspects of learning. It may always be a problem for them to fill in the gaps. None of these children should be labelled remedial, dyslexic or worst of all stupid. They are victims of special circumstances and are probably far from unintelligent. The real difficulty is in recognising such children and then planning how to fill in their gaps. Informed sympathy as well as considerable sensitivity are prerequisites for the teacher, and it may not always be easy. Many children, under such stresses as have been described, are far from easy to deal with. (Neither are their understandably anxious parents.) Clear diagnoses are essential for successful understanding and treatment of complex conditons. Once again handwriting may be a help in diagnosis. There are specific factors that children can focus on in the written trace such as capital letters or the movement of individual letters, or even joins if the child is old enough. It may be possible to assess what has been learned or not, by first scrutinising written work and then by asking a few tactful questions. The children may know only too well the cause of their difficulties, and are often relieved to find a sympathetic listener.

27 Posture as an indicator, as well as a cause of problems

Details of writers' posture can sometimes be as useful an indicator of difficulties as their handwriting itself. People's body language may be as eloquent as any verbal description that they might give, and it is up to the observer to interpret and use this information. Confidence or lack of it is evident before the writer even sits down, and quite a lot can be learned about muscle tone from a casual handshake.

Extremes of height, unusual body proportions or long fingers, for example, are easily noticed and will indicate likely causes of pain to an informed observer. The effect of extreme tension can easily be spotted, particularly when it results in white knuckles or hyperflexed fingers or thumb. Should the tension be affecting muscles further up the arm, it is just as likely to cause pain but it is not so easy to spot through a long-sleeved shirt. The results of such tension can be seen as indentations on the page, but that is not much help in identifying the seat of the tension. If the tension causes too much downward pressure, then this can be observed by watching the flattening of the edge of the hand as it tries to move along the line. The result of too much downward pressure is a build-up of lines on the paper. Letters are superimposed one on another as the hand is unable to make lateral movements. This can also result in uneven writing as the hand jerks along the line, alternately sticking and freeing itself. Once the seat of tension is identified, it will be easier to explain to the writer how to relax the muscles involved. Visible feedback from the written trace will be more useful to the writer when linked to the cause of the tension.

A floppy posture may indicate nothing more serious than boredom, but it can become habitual and end up causing backache or even visual problems. One pupil complained of persistant focussing problems but all relevant tests failed to show anything wrong with his eyes. It was baffling until the writer was seen in action. Then an awkward posture showed how the eyestrain could have been caused. An inappropriate paper position can lead to writers adopting such an uncomfortable posture that backache, headache or cramps of all kinds can result. A diagnosis is more likely to be accurate if the writer's posture is observed and taken into consideration.

What could these two girls' postures indicate? The first one might be just tired or bored, but she could be occluding her left eye because of some visual problem. The left-hander is bending sideways to see what she is writing, because her paper is straight in front of her.

95

Penhold and hands as indicators

Penhold can also reveal a great deal about the writer. It can indicate from a very early age those children at either extreme of development. If you watch a group of pre-school children and observe how they handle their colouring pens, you may get a fair indication of those who will have little trouble with the manipulative aspect of handwriting. Closer observation will often reveal how competent some children are already at devising different holds for different writing or marking tools, and for using them for different purposes, such as outlining or filling in. Young children will vary so much that, while some will be managing bi-manual tasks, others will have hands that seem to resemble a bunch of sausages more than a tool for precise and delicate movements. How observers might use this information would be up to them, but a study of this subject would be likely to add to the argument that children vary considerably in their early graphic development and experience. This leads to a position where it is difficult to advise on such matters as the ideal penhold for a five-year-old child, or to be sure at any age what might be exactly correct for any particular proportion of hand. After an extensive search I have failed to find any substantial research on such essential aspects of writing posture as different hand sizes or proportions.

Observation of hand positions leads to a realisation that they often reflect the different ways that people use their bodies. Some secondary school pupils' unconventional penholds seem to reflect their aggressive attitude to school and to life in general. At the other extreme, an artistically inclined five-year-old already seems to hold the pencil in such a way that suggests that an oval slanting writing will be the result, with the hand delicately balanced on its edge. Undoubtedly good training will help, but observation often suggests how much good writers seem to owe to innate talents and physique. Maybe the converse applies to many poor writers.

Learning from the physically handicapped

The specific treatment of physically handicapped children is beyond the scope of this book. Severe handicaps may make handwriting a low priority for some children. Computer technology may provide more appropriate means of communicating, but to make a personal mark is a basic human need, so handwriting should be encouraged alongside other techniques wherever possible. The purpose of this part of the book is to encourage teachers, therapists and others to learn from observing children. There is much to learn from watching the boundless ingenuity and motivation of physically handicapped children. Observing how well children with considerable hand deformities manage to write perfectly well, often without special aids, can lead to a much wider perspective of penhold. Conventional penhold is a meaningless term for those without the usual complement of fingers, but there are many possible ways of lodging and using a pen. With hands that have little flexibility and cannot hold a pen, two hands working in unison may enable the patient to write. We have a stereotyped idea of how a pen should be used and this aspect of handwriting is discussed at length in Section 16. However if we care to look at what might work for children instead of what we think ought to work, a good place to learn is a classroom of physically handicapped children.

28 An attitude of understanding

Some people may feel that this section of the book is not relevant to the mainstream school. The idea of using handwriting as an indicator, however, would help everyone to develop a deeper understanding of their pupils, and the kind of problems that have been described here are not likely to disappear. Indeed, without going into too many details, it is possible that they may be on the increase. Whilst advancements in medical knowledge have reduced many serious physical handicaps, they have at the same time, directly or indirectly, led to the increase of other less discernable problems. With the survival of many low birth-weight babies, the treatment of previously fatal conditions such as leukaemia and brain tumours, and the ability of spina bifida patients to be happily integrated into mainstream education, teachers face new challenges. Many children in these categories still face considerable difficulties. These may amount to no more than relatively minor but nonetheless tiresome 'differences' in their ability to perform motor or perceptual tasks such as handwriting. In other cases the children may show no outward signs of their problems, but their worries about their physical or medical conditions may well be reflected in their handwriting. An understanding of these matters is likely to be useful in most of our schools.

The final part of this book set out to show how problems show through handwriting, suggesting that the poor writing is the symptom and the teacher needs to search for the reason and then try to prescribe a cure. It is expecting a lot of newly qualified teachers that they should recognise the signs of some of the conditions mentioned here. If the school itself has understood the philosophy behind the argument, then that alone will be a great step forward. With this understanding, children should no longer be blamed for something that they may be unable to remedy. Those who try to overcome complex obstacles by themselves, can be applauded for their ingenuity and perseverance. They can also show us the way to help others in the same situation – if only we will listen to them.

Writing reflects our feelings. You do not need to read the message to see that this boy is in trouble. The message is 'I hate school, man I hate school.'

Index

allergy   93
ascenders   29

Briem, Gunnlaugur SE   8, 10

Callewaert, H.   68–9
capital letters   14, 30
cerebral palsy   89–90
concepts behind alphabet   11–15
co-ordination, poor   76
curriculum planning   25–8
cursive and semi-cursive   31

descenders   29
diagnosis   75–6
directionality   83–5
dyspraxic   76

entry strokes   29
exit strokes   9, 29

Fagg, R.   48
Fairbank, A.   8
fatigue   92–3
furniture   17

gaps in learning   94
Gordon, V.E.C. and Mock, R.   9

hands   21–2, 66–7
handedness   80–2
height differentials   13
hyperactive   94

illegibility   4–5
incorrect movement   43
indicator, handwriting as   95
italic   57–8

joins   23, 32, 44–52

left-handers   11, 19–20, 79–82
legibility   4–5, 24
letter families   12
levels of writing   ii, 2, 5
light   20
lines   20–1

mirror images   13
models   8–9, 32
    effects of   48, 57–8, 73–4
    looking at   53

movement   7
    between letters   45
    of letters   12, 26, 32, 39

name writing   7
neatness   8
Nelson, *New Nelson Teacher's Manual*   8

pain   66–9
paper position   17–18, 70–2
paper size   17–18
parents   7, 10
pen-preference test   63–5
penhold
    as indicator   96
    looking at   66–9
pens and pencils   18, 61–5
perceptual problems   86–8
personal hand   6
point of entry   40
posture   22, 25, 70, 95
pre-school   7, 26
pressure, pen   45
print script   7–8, 30
priorities   25–8

recommendations   73–4
references   36
research methods   34–6
reversal of letters   13
Richardson, Marion   8, 48, 53, 55–6

secondary school   4–5, 27–8, 51, 59, 65
signature   6
slant   21
slanting surface   17, 90
Smith and Inglis   8
spacing   14, 80
speed, of writing   4, 46, 52, 59–60
spelling   77
stroke-related families   12
style   32
surveys   33–4, 41

teachers' handwriting   53–6
tension   78
terminology   29–32
testing   41
tremors   89–91
typefaces   10

visual problems   88

Yevtushenko, Y.   i